= **VITAL SPEECHES OF THE DAY** PRESENTS =

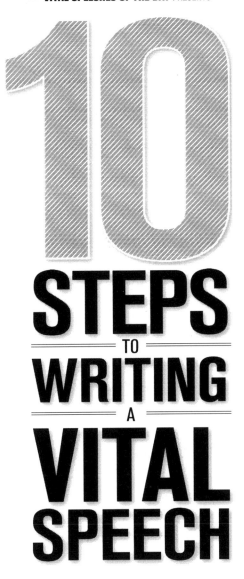

10

STEPS
= TO =
WRITING
= A =
VITAL
SPEECH

ISBN-13: 978-1463742775
ISBN-10:1463742770

Published by *Vital Speeches of the Day*, a McMurry Inc. publication.

Correspondence:
Vital Speeches of the Day
c/o McMurry Inc.
1010 E. Missouri Ave.
Phoenix, AZ 85014
(888) 303-2373
info@vsotd.com

Book Website:
http://www.vsotd.com/10Steps

Printed in U.S.A.

AUTHOR BIO

Fletcher Dean

Fletcher Dean is an award-winning writer of speeches and articles for a wide variety of business, educational and motivational speakers.

He won the Cicero Speechwriting Awards Grand Prize for the best speech of the year in 2008 as well as three other Cicero Awards. He's a four-time presenter at the annual Speechwriting Conference in Washington, D.C.

Dean has more than 20 years' experience as a communications professional. As a speechwriter, annual report writer, journalist and teacher, Dean has written on a broad range of subjects and in a variety of forums. From the National Press Club to the CEO Club of Boston, and from Rio de Janeiro to San Francisco and Washington, his speeches have helped executives and business leaders deliver their ideas to audiences around the world. Those speeches have been reprinted in such prestigious journals as *Vital Speeches of the Day* (13 times), *Executive Speeches*, *Speechwriter's Newsletter* and *Executive Excellence*.

Dean is a graduate of The University of Virginia's College at Wise with a bachelor's degree in English and a concentration in business communications. He also has an MFA in professional writing from Western Connecticut State University. He's the editor of *Grandpap Told Me Tales*, a collection of traditional Appalachian folk tales. ✿

TABLE OF CONTENTS

David Murray

Editor, *Vital Speeches of the Day*

This is not my book on speechwriting. But it is my foreword, and in order to properly introduce you to this peculiar field of practice, I must recall my own introduction to it. I was an English major just emerged from college when I first became aware of the existence of speechwriters and speechwriting.

Before then, I had only two questions about public rhetoric:

Who knows who writes the blather that comes out of the mouths of adults at boring ceremonies I'd never go to? And: Who cares?

But I went to work for a trade publisher that put out a weekly thing called *Speechwriter's Newsletter.*

So I had to care. (Because caring is so much easier than pretending to.)

I expressed my sudden interest in speechwriting in what now seems to be a number of predictable stages: misplaced moral outrage, impossibly condescending pity and emerging admiration.

Larry Ragan, the publisher of *Speechwriter's Newsletter,* used to quote Gertrude Stein or somebody who supposedly said something like, "Some people prefer a moral issue to a real one."

I think Stein meant young people and, if that's the case, it fit me perfectly. I spent lots of my first year or two asking speechwriters where they drew the moral line. Would you write for the CEO of a tobacco company? Can an evil person deliver a truly great speech? Would you write a speech or even a sentence with which you fundamentally disagreed?

"These are interesting questions to discuss on a winter's evening with a bottle of wine," as Larry Ragan also used to say. But day to day ... does a surgeon have either the ability or the time to assess the pros and cons of saving the life of the patient beneath his knife?

Before long, I became bored with the question of the morality of speechwriting and magnanimously decided to allow speechwriters to make their own personal arrangements with God, without the intervention of a 24-year-old English major.

That's when I started to feel sorry for speechwriters.

(Here, I must interrupt to note that during the time I'm talking about, there were many more pure speechwriters than there are today. A big company with a public presence would have a speechwriting *department,* several middle-aged men whose activities ranged from reading, thinking, lunchtime drinking, hammering away at their old typewriters or their new word processors, and smoking pipes. There are still dedicated speechwriters in the world—the author of this book a lucky example, and even he says his executive communication activities are much broader than researching and writing speeches—but most speechwriting these days is done in between news releases and intranet articles, videos and ghost tweets. And it's sober and smoke-free, for better or for worse.)

Speechwriters were usually the most erudite people in the communication department—and often in the whole company. I remember one who had a photographic memory, able to quote long passages of literature from memory; another launched a freelance speechwriting practice with the prize money from winning on *Jeopardy!* To these pre-Internet characters, quotation books were a crutch for lesser-read souls. They were also the most entertaining people in the communication business. A cocktail party at a Speechwriter's Conference was less business networking than an evening at the Algonquin Round Table.

The only interruption in speechwriters' quirky delightfulness, actually, was that they were saying preposterous things. Like, "I don't need a byline." And a separate and even more pitiable claim: "I have no authorial pride." Which meant that they didn't care about what they thought; they didn't even care about the words they wrote. As long as the speech pleased the boss, their professional obligation was complete. And their personal satisfaction? That was irrelevant, so they claimed, even to them.

And so I, a young and ambitious writer whose byline was the happiest sight in the world and whose own ideas were just beginning to form into what I was sure would become a great, impenetrable yet inviting fortress of intellect and culture, felt sorry for the speechwriter.

It took awhile and a number of my own years writing lots of non-bylined stuff for trade newsletters and not for *The New Yorker*—for me to realize that speechwriters were lying.

That they *never* forgot their own ideas. That they *always* tried, though often subconsciously, to push the speaker they were working for—whether the head of a charity or the chairman of an oil company—in the direction of virtue.

Every speech was infused with as much candor, intellectual integrity, humor, humility, warmth—even love—that the speechwriter dared to introduce. And because speeches ultimately serve institutions and not human beings, the speechwriter suffered the extraction of many of those human virtues, draft by agonizing draft.

A hard job. A messy job. An occasionally silly job. (A veteran speechwriter famously said that the client's command to the speechwriter is, "Write down my ideas as if I had them.")

But usually, speechwriting is an admirable job in which full-time speechwriters *do* take pride, and which part-timers consider their most important task.

Recently I asked some speechwriters about the meaning of their work. I asked them whether they thought speechwriting had a "higher social purpose." (I know: That English grad inside me isn't dead yet.)

"Why don't you ask the converse: Does this profession have an insidious purpose?" asked veteran speechwriter Henry Ehrlich, who spent many years writing for big banks. "I still get accosted by acquaintances from my old days in the banking business whose first words are, 'This financial crisis is all your fault.' While I would welcome some checks at the old prices, I'm at peace with myself for the fact that the best speeches I've written in the past few years were for my son's wedding, my niece's wedding and my father's funeral."

"Even great leaders need help composing their thoughts into a conveyable, dynamic format that can be understood and accepted by the masses," said communication veteran Jessica Richardson (who is more typical of today's communication-generalist who writes speeches as a part of her work). "I would posit that without a great speechwriter, there are many great and worthy voices which would have gone unheard."

Communication pro Jim Nichols has been lucky to write primarily for the CEO of "a philanthropic organization with noble intentions." Helping such an organization in any way gives Nichols "pride in knowing, or at least hoping, that my work might have helped accomplish some socially worthy goals." If ever he's faced with the choice to work for an organization whose mission is less clearly good, "perhaps I'll have to wrestle with some existential questions about the worth of what I'm doing. If that time comes, I'll be glad to know I'm not alone."

The main beneficiaries of great speeches aren't speakers, but audiences, says veteran speechwriter Hal Vincent. "Speeches are meant to affect audiences—sometimes well beyond a room. People listening and watching deserve to be informed, entertained, motivated, even inspired. Surely, the higher purpose speechwriting serves is to help speakers convey their thoughts in meaningful ways."

And Boe Workman, a longtime speechwriter for AARP, gives the final word to Isocrates, who said in *The Antidosis*:

> There is no institution devised by man which the power of speech has not helped us establish. For this it is which has laid down laws concerning things just and unjust, and things honorable and base; and if it were not for these ordinances we should not be able to live with one another. It is by this also that we confute the bad and extol the good. Through this we educate the ignorant and appraise the wise; for the power to speak well is taken as the surest index of a sound understanding, and discourse which is true and lawful and just is the outward image of a good and faithful soul. ... We shall find that none of the things that are done with intelligence take place without the help of speech, but that in all our actions as well as in all our thoughts speech is our guide, and it is most employed by those who have the most wisdom.

"There is no higher moral purpose than that!" Workman adds.

With high purpose comes heavy responsibility—to write speeches the very best way you know how.

Written by one of the most experienced, thoughtful, articulate working speechwriters in the world, this book is the best start you could possibly have.

As editor of *Vital Speeches of the* Day—the young English major has come a long way—I very much look forward to reading the first fine speech I know you'll someday be proud to send me. No byline necessary. I'll know.

David Murray, June 21, 2011 ✿

INTRODUCTION:

Who Do YOU Write For?

When I get ready to talk to people, I spend two-thirds of the time thinking what they want to hear and one-third thinking about what I want to say.

– Abraham Lincoln

Want to incite a riot the next time you get more than two speechwriters together in the same room? Ask them who they write for.

Typically, you get responses like "I write for the CEO" or "My principal is the executive vice president for Widget Control" or some other drivel. But that's only partly true. Smart speechwriters know that they serve many masters and the person who's actually signing their checks and giving the speeches is just one of those. In most cases, the speaker isn't even the most important player in a speech event.

Smart speechwriters know that they write primarily for the audience.

Lee Iacocca, one of the greatest business leaders and speakers of the 20th century, put it this way: "If a speaker begins with a deep sense of obligation to the audience, everything else falls into place."

'A Deep Sense of Obligation to the Audience'

Effective speechwriting isn't (only) about making your speaker look great. It isn't (just) about fancy words and clever phrasing. Effective speechwriting is about ensuring the audience's needs and expectations are met. That they are persuaded to follow. That they are enthused about their work and themselves. That they are inspired to think or act differently. In short, that they not only hear the words, but understand and accept the message as their own.

That's the essence of this book. It's a primer on how to write a speech so that the audience not only hears the words (which is part of the struggle) but that they understand them as well (which is more difficult). As such, it is also about one crucial aspect of leadership: the ability to communicate clearly, directly and with a purpose.

What purpose, you ask? Speeches can generally fall into one of five broad audience-centric areas. They can:

1. **Inform:** Offer purpose, direction and vision.

2. **Create Understanding:** Help people understand the reason behind the actions.

3. **Reinforce Shared Values:** Allow people to feel part of a larger group.

4. **Change Attitudes:** Giving people new perspectives so they and their organizations can grow and prosper.

5. **Elicit Action:** The ultimate goal for leaders.

These five areas—what I call the Communication Hierarchy—play a large part in this book. It's not enough for most speeches to simply Inform. If that's your only goal, you can issue an email or distribute a note. No, the ultimate goal for your speaker/leader is to get actions and results. But that won't happen until people have the basic facts (Inform), understand how those facts affect them (Create Understanding), believe they are part of the solution (Reinforce Values), and have the proper mindset (a Changed Attitude). The hierarchy cannot be taken out of sequence. One rung leads on the other.

Speakers often undermine their own position and credibility by either not speaking with a purpose or failing to recognize what their audiences are capable of hearing and responding to. Both are deadly transgressions.

The fact is that people today are impatient. That's true whether the audience is a middle-school soccer team or savvy midlevel managers at a conference show. They want to know how a speaker can help them achieve their own goals. What words does she have that can aid them? How does a speaker's knowledge transfer for their benefit? Failing to recognize this—in other words, failing to speak with the right purpose—is to court calamity and risk alienating the audience. Do it enough times and your speaker could soon lose the very mantle of leadership itself. And, yet, I see it again and again from leaders in all walks of life.

This is where good speechwriters earn their pay. They help keep the focus on the audience and bring leadership communication down to a simple, understandable level. By following the recommendations that follow, you will become a more polished speechwriter and a more valuable part of your organization. You'll be a writer who communicates plainly so that your words are not only heard, but understood and, finally, acted upon.

The real key to accomplishing that is to consider this most critical question about every talk you give and speech you deliver: Who do YOU write for?

A lot of communication failures occur because speechwriters disregard this question and develop messages that serve their speaker's own limited interest without any regard to what the audience needs or wants to hear. Their messages not only come across as dull and boring, but the speakers themselves often seem arrogant and out of touch.

Successful speechwriters, however, understand that audiences have needs, too. Some-times it's as basic as information or direction; sometimes it's something loftier like inspiration. Regardless, speechwriters who understand their audience's needs—and respond to them with carefully chosen words that serve both audience AND speaker—can create magic.

Like all good magic, a well-crafted and well-delivered speech appears seamless to the audience. They don't need to understand the mechanics of the speech. But you do. As a speechwriter, you need to understand how all of the pieces work together so you can build an audience connection so strong that, after the words fade away and the audience members go back to their offices or homes, the ideas linger.

But ... you must understand who you are writing for, what the audience's needs are, what their likes and dislikes are and what they value. So the first step in your journey to learn how to become an effective speechwriter is to assess the audience. ✿

STEP 1:

Know Thy Audience

*Designing a presentation without defining the audience is like addressing
a love letter: "To Whom It May Concern."*

– Gene Zelazny, McKinsey and Co.

Writing a speech is like writing a love letter and then letting someone else read it aloud. You put your heart and soul into the words, you offer it up, hoping it will be accepted, but ... you're never quite sure. Much depends on how the words are interpreted and received (or not). And, let's face it: A lot is on the line with love letters and speeches—your reputation, your respect, and your ego.

It's hard enough to write a love letter to someone you know, you've talked with and who knows you. But at least in those situations you have some idea of that person's likes and dislikes, what that person's background is and maybe, if you know the person well, what his or her hopes and dreams are. Imagine, as Gene Zelazny points out, how difficult it would be to write a love letter to a total stranger. Or worse, imagine writing a love letter and having it read aloud to a few hundred strangers.

No one would purposely do that. Yet, so many speechwriters do essentially the same thing every day. They spend countless hours researching the topic, solitarily poring over their copy, fine-tuning each phrase and carefully crafted analogy until—finally—when the speech is polished and approved, they hand it over to a speaker who will walk into a ballroom in another city and deliver the lines. And at no time during the process have they asked the fundamental question: Who's listening?

They write their words long in advance, not knowing what the hot topics of the day will be. They haven't researched the ballroom. They don't know the seating arrangement. They haven't talked with a conference organizer to get an understanding of the audience's likes and dislikes. And—no surprise—their speakers leave the podium without knowing what effect their words might have had on the audience.

Think of it as the "me, me, me" talk because the writers who craft these talks give so much attention to their organization's own needs that they forget about the needs of the audience.

A good speech, like a good love letter, is warm and personal. Recipients feel like it was written and delivered just for them. And they return that warmth with attention and

9

respect. How do you achieve that level of warmth and personalization? By asking questions. Before you write any words—even before your speaker has agreed to speak at any event—you should ask lots and lots of questions.

There are three potential areas you need to explore before you accept a speaking invitation or begin putting pen to paper. You need to gather information about:

* The audience

* The purpose of the event

* The situational factors surrounding the event.

It all starts with the audience

President Abraham Lincoln once said that when he prepared for a speech, he spent two-thirds of his time thinking about what the audience wanted to hear and one-third of his time thinking about what he wanted to say. Like Iacocca, Lincoln understood that one secret to getting audiences to listen is to write something they want to hear and by giving it to them in a way they can understand.

Here's an example of doing it the wrong way. Let's say you work with the chief financial officer of a large manufacturing company. One day a former professor invites the CFO back to his alma mater to speak about his job. Simple enough, right? It's a college group and you assume the crowd will be a bunch of undergraduate finance and business majors. You don't want to get over their heads so you write some general comments, confident the CFO will be able to answer any question that might come his way. And maybe, if you've thought about it, you might ask your own college-aged child for the name of a current music group you could throw in, just to show that your speaker is still hip.

When the CFO arrives at the auditorium where your talk is being held, though, you discover the audience isn't undergraduates. It's actually a meeting of business and accounting professors from across the country. They're not interested in the generalities you prepared—they're interested in the complex financial models you use to run your business. Instead of a business overview, the CFO is expected to share with them how the company uses hedge funds to manage foreign currency risks and they want to know how the latest regulations from the Securities and Exchange Commission affected the company's most recent financial report, which all of them have read in detail, of course.

The speech is still about what the CFO does at work. Then again, it's not, is it?

Remember that every time your principal speaks, his or her leadership is being judged. People are watching, people are listening and people are forming opinions about what they see and hear. Why risk that leadership position by not doing the homework ahead of time?

For a speech or presentation to be successful, you need to talk *to the individuals* in the audience about ideas and concepts they're interested in. How else will you tell relevant stories and build examples around themes with which they're familiar?

But even before that, you need to know if there's a match between what you might write and what they might want to hear. And the only effective way for you to find that information is by taking the time—before you even accept an invitation to speak—to do a deep analysis of the audience. There are two aspects of every audience that deserve some attention.

For each speech, you need to consider the audience's demographic and psychographic characteristics. Each will be important and give you vital clues to help paint a vivid picture of what you're facing. Depending on how much time you have and the resources available, you may get more or less information than you need. But a little background information is better than none and will move you far ahead in determining whether to speak to the audience.

DEMOGRAPHICS – Exploring the audience demographics is the first step. Break down your analysis into topics such as these:

- AGE – Each audience will have an age range that will dictate the kind of humor you can use, how experienced they are and what cultural references they are familiar with and you can use with confidence.

- GENDER – Would you use a football analogy with a predominantly female crowd? Maybe, but probably not. How about giving a list of ingredients in facial makeup to highlight your speech on the dangers of chemicals to a mostly male audience? There are most likely better examples you could use.

- RACIAL/ETHNIC/CULTURAL BACKGROUNDS – The cultural references for these various audiences will guide your research and remarks. A mixed crowd is one thing; a predominantly Latino crowd may be another, requiring a different approach.

- SOCIOECONOMICS – This may vary widely or be amazingly homogeneous. At the very least it will determine the focus of your comments and will most likely guide your examples, your speech patterns and even your dress.

- EDUCATIONAL BACKGROUND – It's not wise to assume everyone is similar to you, which is the way many people think of audiences. A quick review may reveal some interesting tidbits that could guide your use of jargon, terminology, words and phrasing.

- RELIGION – Faith may be a factor, depending on the type of talk you're writing. (But tread lightly on religious topics unless you're specifically writing a talk on that subject or you know the audience extremely well and know they will respond positively to your religious references.)

- COMMON GROUP MEMBERSHIPS – Would most audience members be Democrats, Republicans or some other political party? Perhaps they're members of the American Civil Liberties Union or most belong to a labor union. Knowing whom they associate with as individuals is vitally important.

- **WORK TITLES** – This is especially important in corporate and large organizational settings. If the audience members are all C-suite members (CEO, COO, CFO, CIO, CTO, etc.), the talk will be different—or at least *should* be different—than if they all have "Manager" in their title.

PSYCHOGRAPHIC – Knowing the demographics will also go a long way in helping you determine the audience members' psychographics—their over-arching beliefs, values and attitudes. Here, you'll want to divide your analysis into three broad areas:

- **GENERAL BELIEFS AND ATTITUDES** – Most audiences will share a similar set of beliefs and values. After all, they're all gathered together for some purpose and many times it's their shared belief system. An example might be a political rally where the audience members have come together specifically because they are all Democrats or all support a specific cause. Or perhaps your principal has been asked to go around the community giving pep talks for a new fundraising event. It will benefit you as a writer—and your speaker—if you realize that not every audience you speak to in the city thinks the same, has the same background or same value system. Tailoring the remarks accordingly will help your speaker connect as a leader by earning respect from the audience.

- **ATTITUDES AND BELIEFS TOWARD THE SUBJECT** – Even when people belong to a particular group, they rarely agree on every issue. Some topics are divisive, so knowing how the audience feels toward the subject will help determine whether you have something to share with them. This is the time to ask someone close to the event questions like these: What interests this audience most or least? How familiar are they with the topic? When was the last time someone spoke about this subject to them and what was the response?

- **ATTITUDES AND BELIEFS TOWARD THE SPEAKER** – Does your speaker already have a reputation or particular credibility with this audience? Is the speaker familiar to the audience members or has he or she spoken to them before? The audience will have some attitude about your speaker, even if it's no more than what's presented in a conference brochure three months before the talk or what's passed around on the grapevine. Never underestimate that prior reputation. A good speechwriter will know what those beliefs are before accepting the invitation to speak because having credibility ahead of time is vital to delivering a persuasive talk. If your speaker doesn't have credibility, there may still be time to get it before the actual speech.

What's the purpose?

Just as every audience is different, every speaking opportunity will have a different purpose. Some are academic in nature while others are more commercial. The speech might be given in the office, the ball field or a church. Some opportunities have serious undertones; others are light. But you won't know unless you ask about the details:

- **PURPOSE** – The purpose of speaking opportunities can vary greatly but often fall into one of these broad categories: academic, commercial, political, fundraising, entertaining and motivational.

- **AGENDA** – Ask for the agenda—even a tentative agenda—ahead of time. It will give you insight into the tone of the event and who the other speakers are.

- **EVENT FREQUENCY** – Many speaking opportunities are regular events. Knowing this helps because you can look back at previous agendas, speakers and topics. You might even contact a previous speaker who can give you valuable insights about the event and the audience. If it's not an annual event, ask why it's being held now.

- **OTHER SPEAKERS** – Knowing who else is speaking—and where they appear on the agenda—can provide clues about the expected audience, the overall tone of the event and your place at the event. It will also give you a chance to consider what others are saying and ensure the remarks you write are unique.

- **YOUR SPEAKER'S ROLE** – It's critical that you ask ahead of time what's expected of your speaker and what his or her role will be. Many times, your principal may be the featured speaker at a plenary session in front of all attendees. Other times, the event may have breakout sessions where the speaker's role is to address a subset of the entire audience. Then again, the speaker may be part of a panel and expected to make five to 10 minutes' worth of comments and then take questions. These circumstances all dramatically impact the way you research and write. For instance, a panel opportunity is more likely to be one in which your speaker simply presents information; a keynote opportunity may be a chance to be more persuasive.

- **QUESTION/ANSWER PERIOD** – Your speaker may be expected to hang around after the talk to answer questions from the audience or a moderator. Knowing this will help you prepare a list of likely questions and suggested answers that are part of the speech package you deliver to your speaker.

- **MEDIA ATTENDANCE** – Leaders are often asked to speak at community functions, fundraising events and before boards and councils. Some of those events are magnets for the media, and some event organizers specifically invite media. It pays to ask ahead of time so you're not surprised when lines from the speech are in the newspaper the next day. If the media will be there, you can write with reporters squarely in mind and increase the likelihood that the words come off well in the newspaper or on TV.

What is your speaker walking into?

A good situational analysis of what your speaker is walking into can often be the difference between amazing success and stunning failure. Many talks have been ruined because no one thought to ask some basic questions of *when, where* and *how*. The last step in this pre-work phase will help you review all of those small details. Here are some things to look for:

* **LOCATION** – Where will the event be held? Look beyond just city and state. Which part of the city, which building, which room? It's important to be as specific as you can to minimize surprises. If your speaker is the manager in a manufacturing company and asked to speak about quality issues, it makes a difference if the event location is a conference room or an ad hoc stage set up on the manufacturing floor. The distractions are different, the tone is different and your principal's persona as a leader will be different in different locations. A simple example: You wouldn't wear a business suit to the manufacturing floor where the rest of the audience is in coveralls. So ask. If the event is part of a larger event, you can also do some research to see what's happening around the location where you're speaking that may aid your talk. A nod to outside events—which will be on the minds of the audience—is usually appreciated. It shows you've noticed and you care.

* **TIME OF DAY** – Here's an incredibly important detail you don't want to overlook. Speeches and presentations have different requirements depending on when they're delivered.

    * *Morning speeches* have audiences that are more awake, more eager to learn and generally more receptive to your messages. You can get away with a fairly serious talk here and be forgiven, even if your content is not "wow-factor" great.

    * *Lunchtime speeches* are universally strict on their time requirements so be careful to find out when the meeting will adjourn and plan your remarks accordingly. It's usually more important to be brief here as people on their lunch breaks are anxious to return to work.

    * *Afternoon speeches* generally have audiences that are less awake. They have that post-lunch malaise that makes any serious topic difficult to deliver. It's also the time of day when their thoughts might turn to unanswered emails and work back at the office. Entertaining speeches work well here as do speeches with material that's packaged as short, snappy segments.

Lower the lights for a slide show at your own risk during an afternoon speech, unless your intent is to provide the audience some peaceful napping time.

- *Dinner and after-dinner speeches* are notoriously difficult. Many times the audience members will have consumed alcohol and will be less attentive. Other times, they're anxious to get on with the evening's events and have less patience. If your speaker is strong on humor, now is the time to show off a little. If not, brevity rules.

- **ROOM DETAILS**—If possible, get a diagram of the speaking room ahead of time. Is it long and narrow or broad and shallow? The difference will affect the kind of slides you prepare if you're doing an electronic presentation or if you have visuals. You'll also want to know:

  - Your speaker's location immediately before and after speaking;

  - Whether there will be a podium and where it will be;

  - How the lighting is arranged and whether your speaker will have enough light at the podium to see his notes;

  - What kind of sound system is being used;

  - What kind of microphone is available. If your speaker likes to walk around during the presentation, be sure a wireless microphone is available;

  - What the audiovisual capabilities are and whether you should bring a projector if you're developing an electronic presentation; and

  - The name and phone number of the person who will be available if you or your speaker has technical difficulties.

Bringing it all together

The whole point of doing a strict pre-acceptance analysis of the audience, the event and the overall situation is to determine some basic information:

1. Will speaking at this event help further your speaker's personal goals as a leader or the goals of the organization being represented? Unless you've done the analysis, you won't know the answer to this question. There must be a match between your message and the audience. If you don't examine that relationship, you'll be addressing your love letter "To Whom it May Concern."

2. What kind of talk do you need to write? Does your talk need to be humorous and light or serious and sobering? Will you need to write 10 minutes' worth of remarks or 60 minutes? Will the audience respond to the jokes and anecdotes you've used in the past, or do you need fresh material?

3. What are the small details that will separate success from failure? Even well-written speeches can be ruined by the smallest of details. A loud construction job outside of the speaking forum can doom a speech, especially if a good microphone isn't available. The unconscious message is that your speaker can't speak above the noise, a fatal flaw for any leader. Likewise, a slide presentation with detailed graphs and small type will be useless to those sitting in the back of a large auditorium and send the message that your speaker either doesn't care or hasn't done his homework. Again, both undermine leadership.

Does this type of analysis take time? Yes. Is it worth it? Absolutely. The main thing to remember is that a speech is rarely about just your speaker and your message. It's also about making sure your message reaches the right audience with the right emphasis and in the right way. It has to be warm and personal so they all walk away thinking the remarks were prepared and delivered just for them. It works for good love letters, and it works for good speeches and presentations, too. ✿

INSIDER TIPS

#1 Conference organizers can be your best friend when doing a pre-speech analysis. They probably already have statistics and background on the audience and may be able to give you specific information about the location. Play nice with them and it will advance your cause immeasurably.

#2 If you write a lot or manage a group of speakers, you might want to use a form similar to the one provided here that you can simply fill out with all of the audience analysis questions as a prompt when you're doing your research. This sheet should be the first sheet in your file and be used to provide context when you send the speech up for review.

#3 The first thing to do when you arrive at the speaking event is find the hotel or building support staff and get the name and phone number of someone who can help if things go wrong with the technology.

EVENT ANALYSIS CHECKLIST

Speaker:

Name of Sponsoring Organization:

Primary Contact:

   Phone: Email: Fax:

Event:

Theme:

Location: Event Date:

Time:

   Speaking Slot Date/Time:

Type of Presentation (keynote/panel/Q&A):

   If panel, other speakers:

Question/Answer Planned?

   Moderator: Time:

Other **Confirmed** Speakers:

Other **Requested** Speakers:

Media Promotion?

Media Invited? Confirmed?

Type/Size of Room:

Seating arrangement?

A/V availability?

AUDIENCE PROFILE CHECKLIST

Anticipated Size: Age Range:

Work Titles / Backgrounds (Attendee list available?):

Key Stakeholders (Donors/Customers/Alumni/etc.):

Political Orientation:

Frequency of Meetings: Weekly/Monthly/Annual/Other?

Previous Speakers and Topics:

Upcoming Speakers and Topics:

What topics have been most interesting in the past? Why?

Least interesting topics?

Special concerns/interests for this audience?

Who/What will proceed the speech? Agenda available?

Who/What will follow the speech?

Who will introduce the speaker?

Phone: Email: Fax:

STEP 2:

Aim First, Then Shoot—
Targeting Your Words

Communication ... always makes demands. It always demands that the recipient
become somebody, do something, believe something. It always appeals to motivation.
If, in other words, communication fits in with the aspirations, the values, the purposes
of the recipient, it is powerful. If it goes against his aspirations, his values, his
motivations, it is likely not to be received at all or, at best, to be resisted.

– Peter Drucker, management consultant and author

When I was a kid, my room was plastered with posters of all kinds. Baseball stars. Movie posters. Blacklight posters of tigers and peace signs. (Yeah, it was the 1970s.) But there was one that spoke directly to communication in the modern era. It was funny and—like a lot of good humor—drove straight to the heart of the problem. It said this: *I know that you believe you heard what you think I said, but I'm not sure you realize that what you heard is not what I meant.*

It's OK. You can read it two or three times if you want because it highlights a problem that's endemic with speeches today: The message is confusing.

When it comes to writing effective speeches, the message is paramount. And yet, so few writers actually go through a formal process of identifying not only what the message is, but what they want the message *to do*. Those are two critical questions that you must answer early in the process. And typically, you have to answer the second question before the first. In other words, you have to know what you want the audience to do (or believe) before you can actually know which words will trigger that action.

If you've done the first step of audience analysis, you already have a good idea of what the audience is interested in. You'll know what its beliefs are, what its comfort level is with your speaker and your organization, and you'll have an idea of what its attitudes are, relative to your subject matter.

The next step is to find the connection between where the audience is and what *you* hope to accomplish. The most important thing to remember is that the speechwriter—or the speaker, for that matter—rarely gets to dictate what the audience is ready to do. The audience decides that. If they're not ready to jump in the direction you want, they won't

... and the speech or presentation will seem like a disappointment, perhaps even damaging to your goals and your speaker's leadership.

For successful talks or speeches, you should first determine what the audience is capable of and build messages to fit. Constructing messages before you know what the audience is ready to hear can be disastrous.

Audience analysis will tell you what audiences are capable of hearing. Your job as a speechwriter is now to match your goals with theirs, using the five-step communication hierarchy. There are generally five levels of communication possibilities speakers can achieve with their audiences.

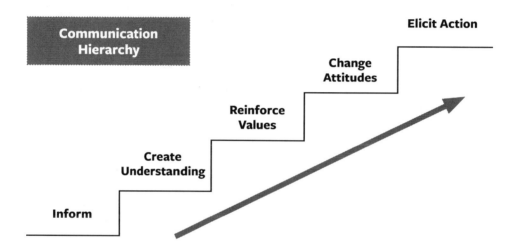

Inform

These speeches are critical for most organizations and the bread and butter of most communications. Organizations have information to share, and speeches—even small ones in front of a dozen people—are a great way to do that because they put people in front of people.

Speeches that fall into this category are generally noncontroversial. They generally answer the basics of: Who, What, When, Where and perhaps How. A great example is when a business wants to announce that everyone in the organization is getting a pay raise. If the pay raise is a good and fair one, the speaker can tell who is getting it, what it will be and when it will be implemented. The audience might have questions about how the raise was configured but, being a fair, across-the-board raise, the answer is noncontroversial.

The speaker or presenter here isn't as important as the message. Most organizations, therefore, can usually allow lower-level staff members or managers to deliver this information.

Create Understanding

This second level of communications is the one that answers a basic question: Why? Let's take the pay-raise scenario and tweak it a bit. In the new scenario, everyone is still getting a pay raise but the raise itself won't take effect as soon as the workers might have expected. A natural question—and the one that must be answered—is why.

Now the messenger becomes just as important as the message. The speaker must have credibility with the audience for this type of communication to be accepted. The speaker must be seen as honest and straightforward.

Another example is when an organization has made a decision it must explain to the community. The local school board might have decided to close a community school and bus the kids to a larger school. An employer might be closing down and laying off workers. The audience will want to know *Why?* And they'll want to hear the explanation from someone they can trust—a leader.

It's important in these situations to provide enough time and the right atmosphere to receive feedback from the audience. Therefore, you need to write in time pauses so your speaker can take questions from the audience. It's also very useful to anticipate the most common and difficult questions and prepare answers ahead of time so the organization's responses are well thought out and complete.

Reinforce Values

This is the classic pep rally speech. At this level, there's really no misunderstanding between the audience and the presenter (or organization). There is only a need to reinforce the values you already share. A typical example is when an organization—usually a community organization like United Way—announces a new fundraising goal. Every year, United Way organizations across the United States hold community meetings to announce their goals and to encourage their individual campaign leaders. These leaders already share United Way's philosophy and principles so this is less about Informing or Creating Understanding, it's about rallying them together toward a common purpose.

This type of speech is one often used by political candidates, too. At campaign stop after campaign stop, they meet with audiences that mostly reflect their own values. They often state their positions on various issues and tell the audience why they are running. But most of the time the main goal is to rally the faithful, get them enthused about the election and make sure they feel like they're part of something larger than themselves.

Change Attitudes

Sometimes, however, speakers actually do have to convince the nonbelievers or fence straddlers. This is the fourth level on the communication hierarchy and a difficult one to do, especially in one talk. Imagine meeting a politician you've never heard of and being asked to vote for him or her after the first meeting. Most people wouldn't do it. First they have to become aware of the candidate (Inform), understand what the candidate stands for and why he or she is running (Create Understanding), and be comfortable that the candidate shares their own values (Reinforce Values) before they'll actually say they'll vote for the candidate.

There are two prerequisites that must exist before a speaker attempts to attain this level of communication with the audience. First, you must have done enough audience analysis to understand in subtle detail what the audience already believes. Secondly, the speaker must be able to state in a single sentence the attitude you want to change. If you can't write it in a single sentence, you may not be ready for this level.

A common example might be the issue of climate change. There are probably dozens of speeches given every week—perhaps every day—about the subject of climate change. The audience could be any company, any business conference center or any other public forum. But what's the specific message? Is it that the science of climate change is solid? Or perhaps that climate change has the potential to impact our daily lives? Notice that neither of those is about Changing Attitudes; they're about informing. The attitude you might want to change, in this case, might be fairly straightforward: Climate change is real.

Paring the attitude you want to change down to one simple sentence is a great way to focus not only your research and writing, it's a great way for speakers to drive to the heart of the issue and show insight and decisiveness. They know what needs to be done and they communicate it, two hallmarks of great leadership (and great speechwriting).

Elicit Action

The holy grail of communication, actually getting someone to do something, stands at the top of the heap for speakers. It's nice if you can Inform an audience, it's good if you can Create Understanding among the audience or Reinforce Shared Values, and it's great if you can Change Attitudes. But none of those carry as much benefit as getting someone to take action.

But this level is also the most difficult to achieve. We all have a great tendency toward inertia. As humans, we're comfortable doing either nothing or doing the same thing we've been doing. Habits turn into routines and routines into ruts. To change attitudes and do something different simply isn't in our nature.

It's like the old story about the five frogs sitting on a log in the forest. If four frogs decide to jump off, how many would be left on the log? The answer: Five, because there's a big difference between deciding and doing.

For speechwriters, getting your audience to jump off the proverbial log is difficult but it also pays the largest dividends. Manufacturers and businesses want people to work safely, for example, and it costs a lot less to persuade them to follow safety rules than deal with the consequences after someone gets injured. Politicians are thrilled if poll numbers show that voters believe and like them. But what they really need is action—they need people to show up on election day and vote for them. Parents want kids who not only understand the logical consequences of drinking and driving, but who can also withstand the pressures that come with being a teen and not put themselves in situations where drinking and driving is even possible.

As a speechwriter, you need to understand each of these levels and prepare your remarks accordingly. Before you can connect with your audience—whether that audience is a community group, the workers in your organization or even your child—you need to decide what you're trying to accomplish and what your audience is ready to listen to.

How to Develop Your Key Messages

Knowing what you're going to say before you start writing is not only a way to crystallize your thinking, it will save you time and effort when you begin writing. But each level on the communication hierarchy carries its own constraints when it comes to building key messages. You'll want to limit the number and type of key messages depending on which level you're targeting. A general rule of thumb is this: the fewer the key messages, the better.

- **INFORMATIVE:** These presentations can usually include any number of key messages (examples: Top 10 Health Concerns or 15 Most Important Political Figures of the 20th Century). Just remember that the more key messages you offer, the more difficult each will be for your audience to remember. You might prepare a document you can share with them—a handout or brochure—that summarizes all of the key points. Regardless of how many messages you have, try to connect them under one larger, umbrella message.

- **CREATE UNDERSTANDING:** Successful speechwriters who try to create understanding will use fewer messages, not more. In fact, you should use the least number possible and absolutely no more than three. Audiences have trouble following more than three substantive messages.

- **REINFORCE SHARED VALUES:** The key message here is that your speaker and the audience are alike and share the same goals. (Example: When potential presidential candidates go to early caucus states on speaking tours, they don't directly ask for support. The purpose is to increase their name recognition and to show that they share the concerns of the audience by reinforcing their shared values. "I'm one of you.") The more values your speaker can reinforce the better, but you can accomplish a lot by knowing ahead of time the two or three that are most important to the audience.

- **CHANGING ATTITUDES:** Like the level above, the fewer messages the better but no more than three. It's always helpful to have supporting points developed for a potential question/answer period.

- **ELICIT ACTION:** There is usually only one key action you're targeting at this level: donate ... volunteer ... vote. Write it down in a single sentence. Focusing on more than one dilutes your message and confuses the audience.

So you know how many key messages to develop, but how do you actually do it? Here's one great trick: Think like a newspaper reporter. I call it the Headline Approach to Developing Messages.

The idea is very simple. Pretend you're a newspaper reporter covering your speech or presentation for the next day's paper. If you were writing the newspaper headline that reported on your talk, what would it say? Write it down, just like you'd like it to appear in the newspaper. Now you're looking at your first and most important key message.

The approach works for three reasons.

First, newspaper headlines are mostly limited to one simple statement. Sometimes it's not even a sentence. But it's always direct and attempts to sum up a speech or event in one easy-to-understand line. And frankly, this may be the *only* thing your audience takes away. So thinking of your key message in one line focuses all of your notes and papers into a single point and has a way of clearing the mind.

Secondly, it works because it forces you to look at the speech or presentation from the eyes of the audience. How will they hear the words? What will they say when someone asks them: "What was that speech about?" Having that perspective as a writer is important.

Finally, this approach generally makes writers (and speakers) push their own goals forward more than they might otherwise. Let me explain. Newspaper headlines invariably focus on action. They center on what happened at an event and not the small details. So if the headline you write sounds something like "Joe Smith Outlines 15-Step Process for Fighting Nail Fungus" you might want to consider putting more action into it. You may, in fact, be giving a speech on fighting nail fungus and have 15 steps people can take. But more focus is always better than less. In this example, all 15 steps probably aren't equal. There may be one more important than the others. So the headline—after focusing your approach—might be "Proper Nutrition Critical in Fighting Nail Fungus."

Principles of Persuasive Writing

Getting others to accept a leader's point of view is the crux of building a successful argument in your speech. Whether you're reinforcing values, trying to elicit action or creating understanding, the audience must be influenced by what you say. And to be influenced, they must believe you. There are three categories of proof that drive believability and the art of persuasion:

- Logic (or reason)

- Emotion

- Character

LOGIC – Most speeches and presentations have some amount of logic built into them. And many speakers—especially those who come from science and technology fields— often rely heavily on the power of logic to influence their arguments. Logic is very good when you're working at the bottom part of the Communication Hierarchy: Informing, Reinforcing Values and Creating Understanding, especially for those audience members who aren't familiar with your topic. If you plan to use this lever, make sure your facts and evidence are sound and your speaker can present it in a straightforward manner.

By itself, however, appealing to logic is rarely effective if your goal is to Change Attitudes or Elicit Action. To change someone's attitude, for example, you first have to accept the fact that they already have one belief and that the belief was probably built, at least partly, on logic itself. There are, as the saying goes, at least two sides to every issue. Two well-meaning and well-educated people can often have vastly different views on the same subject based on their own reasoning. What's a writer to do? It's a poor craftsman (or speechwriter) who has only one tool in the old tool belt. Fortunately, there are two more ways to persuade an audience.

EMOTION – When the goal of your speech or presentation is to get someone to act or to change their attitudes or beliefs, using an emotional approach is often the best technique. United Way uses this approach, for example, when they ask for time and money. They often show videos and use heart-stirring testimonials from people who have been helped by United Way.

To be most effective, emotional appeals must be as specific and vivid as possible. They must use language and images that are emotionally interesting. And they are best used in conjunction with other emotional appeals.

There is a caveat here, however. Audiences will resent any attempt to use this lever to reinforce negative stereotypes or stress negative emotions such as fear and contempt. As a writer, also avoid using an emotional appeal to oversimplify a complex argument. Your audience will see through your attempts and the entire speech could backfire.

CHARACTER – Whether it helps or hurts, your speaker's character is a part of every speech and presentation he or she will give. People will either know the speaker and the speaker's reputation, or not. Either way, that influences the way the audience will react. Character can carry many benefits if you can relay to the audience that the speaker:

* Knows what he or she is talking about.

* Is a reasonable person willing to listen, discuss and compromise (even conceding certain points).

* Is an ethical person with high morals.

* Is concerned about the issues and cares about the audience.

You can certainly convey much of that in the body of the speech itself. The speaker can share part of that with his body language (by smiling and presenting an open posture). You can also build character by ensuring the introduction of the speaker at the podium reinforces all of the things that drive positive images of the speaker's character and show that the person is well-qualified to speak on the issue.

A final word about character: Speakers can actually borrow credibility and increase their own character appeal by the material you choose to include in the speech. Is the speech before a religious organization? A few religious citations will enhance credibility and character.

A speech to a largely NASCAR audience? Why not quote one of the legends of car racing or share an anecdote that reinforces your speaker's connection to the sport? Small insertions like this can improve your speaker's character, credibility and persuasiveness and reinforce his or her ability to be persuasive and, ultimately, to lead. ✿

INSIDER TIPS

#1 The most successful speechwriters will do a check step after developing their key points to see if they have answered the one question every audience member will be asking as they sit waiting for the speaker to finish talking: What's in it for me? If you haven't answered that one question, you may need to revisit your key message points. Remember that most audience members—in their heart—want one of three things in life. They want to be healthier, wealthier or happier. Through your speaker, your goal is to help them achieve at least one of those. Achieve all three and you've hit the jackpot!

#2 Speakers can't take the five levels of communication hierarchy out of order. You must be able to Create Understanding before you Reinforce Values, you must Reinforce Values before you Change Attitudes and you must Change Attitudes before you Elicit Action. And at the base, the audience has to know the facts and be Informed. It's very difficult to accomplish all five levels in one speech.

SPEECH EXAMPLE

Robert F. Kennedy's demonstrated leadership

In 1968, Robert F. Kennedy was a presidential candidate, trying to recover the office that had once been his brother's. He traveled the country talking to large and small groups about the issues that meant the most to them: poverty, civil rights, and racial and economic issues. As a U.S. senator, he had endeared himself to many African-Americans by championing the issues of the disaffected.

Less than a month after declaring his candidacy for president, he was scheduled to make a campaign stop in Indianapolis, Ind. The largely African American crowd had been gathering for hours before Kennedy arrived. Earlier in the day, the charismatic activist and prominent leader of the African-American civil rights movement, Martin Luther King, Jr., had been assassinated.

As Kennedy approached the stage—a flatbed truck—he asked an aide if the crowd knew about the assassination. They didn't. And it was left to him to share the news. Already throughout the United States, the news of the assassination had resulted in mass rioting. Kennedy knew that what he said would impact the way this crowd behaved. The result of his words? Indianapolis was the only major city with a large African-American population to avoid the kind of rioting that plagued other cities in the aftermath of King's death.

This speech is not only a great example of speaking with a purpose, it's a fantastic example—and one of only two I know of—where the speaker covers the entire communication hierarchy in one speech.

SEN. ROBERT F. KENNEDY
ON THE DEATH OF MARTIN LUTHER KING
INDIANAPOLIS, IND.
APRIL, 4, 1968

Ladies and Gentlemen—I'm only going to talk to you just for a minute or so this evening. Because I have bad news for you, for all of our fellow citizens and people who love peace all over the world, and that is that Martin Luther King was shot and killed tonight.

Martin Luther King dedicated his life to love and to justice for his fellow human beings, and he died because of that effort.

In this difficult day, in this difficult time for the United States, it is perhaps well to ask what kind of a nation we are and what direction we want to move in. For those of you who are black—considering the evidence evidently is that there were white people who were responsible—you can be filled with bitterness, with hatred, and a desire for re-

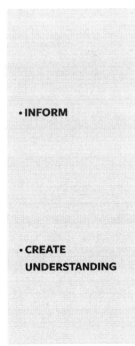

• INFORM

• CREATE
UNDERSTANDING

venge. We can move in that direction as a country, in great polarization—black people amongst black, white people amongst white, filled with hatred toward one another.

Or we can make an effort, as Martin Luther King did, to understand and to comprehend, and to replace that violence, that stain of bloodshed that has spread across our land, with an effort to understand with compassion and love.

For those of you who are black and are tempted to be filled with hatred and distrust at the injustice of such an act, against all white people, I can only say that I feel in my own heart the same kind of feeling. I had a member of my family killed, but he was killed by a white man. But we have to make an effort in the United States ... we have to make an effort to understand, to go beyond these rather difficult times.

My favorite poet was Aeschylus. He wrote: "In our sleep, pain which cannot forget falls drop by drop upon the heart until, in our own despair, against our will, comes wisdom through the awful grace of God."

What we need in the United States is not division; what we need in the United States is not hatred; what we need in the United States is not violence or lawlessness; but love and wisdom, and compassion toward one another, and a feeling of justice toward those who still suffer within our country, whether they be white or whether they be black.

So I shall ask you tonight to return home, to say a prayer for the family of Martin Luther King, that's true, but more importantly to say a prayer for our own country, which all of us love—a prayer for understanding and that compassion of which I spoke.

We can do well in this country. We will have difficult times; we've had difficult times in the past; we will have difficult times in the future. It is not the end of violence; it is not the end of lawlessness; and it is not the end of disorder.

But the vast majority of white people and the vast majority of black people in this country want to live together, want to improve the quality of our life, and want justice for all human beings who abide in our land.

Let us dedicate ourselves to what the Greeks wrote so many years ago: to tame the savageness of man and make gentle the life of this world.

Let us dedicate ourselves to that, and say a prayer for our country and for our people.

- **REINFORCE VALUES**

- **CHANGE ATTITUDES**

- **ELICIT ACTION**

STEP 3:

What Are You Going to Say?
Finding the Right Material

It usually takes more than three weeks to prepare a good impromptu speech.

– Mark Twain, U.S. humorist, writer and lecturer

Successful speeches take a lot of time. Not to write, necessarily. For most people, writing a speech doesn't take nearly as long as researching it. That's why it's important to know ahead of time *what* you need to research. In fact, that was the one of the crucial outcomes of the previous chapter—identifying your key messages so you'll have a guide to focus your research. Now that you have that guide, you're ready to begin gathering information that will make your speech or presentation more believable, more interesting and more engaging for the audience. Remember: One key to getting your message understood is getting the audience to listen.

The object during this phase is not to collect the most material. Instead, you should focus on gathering the most *useful* material in the most efficient manner. Therefore, it's best to divide your research into three buckets. The first two are buckets you'll fill before the talk; the third is one you'll fill—as needed—afterward.

Bucket One: The Pre-write

The best place to start your research is by gathering some basic topical and situational information that will help define the parameters of your speech or presentation.

- **TOPICAL** – You need to discover very quickly what the latest thinking is on your topic. If you're already an authority, you may know the basic arguments. But it always helps to do a quick Internet and magazine search to see what has been said recently. Some questions you'll need to ask include:

  - Are any new elements of the topic being discussed?

  - How divisive are the issues surrounding the topic?

  - Who is the leading (or most popular) expert on the field and what has that person said recently?

- Are there any new books on the subject and what are their main theses?

- Are there any recent news items that might impact the audience's attitudes on this subject? (Hint: Don't just look at your local or national news. Make sure you look at the news sources where the audience hails from.)

■ **SITUATIONAL** – One of the most overlooked areas of research is the situational aspect of the talk. But doing this research will help tremendously if you're able to build it back into the speech later. It will help build your speaker's character and credibility with the audience by showing that he or she cared enough to dig out the small details. Here are some common areas where you can do some quick situational research:

  - **GENERAL LOCATION** – Research some basic facts about the location. If the speech is in Chicago to a mostly local audience, for example, you can gain valuable audience appreciation (and enhance your speaker's character) if your speaker is knowledgeable of happenings in their city. Has the weather been extreme? Mention it. Has there been a major sporting event that your audience may have been aware of? You can possibly work it in. If the audience is traveling in for a conference, you can do similar research by investigating the hotel, the city's history of colorful characters or even sports teams.

  - **SPECIFIC LOCATION** – You must get specific. If you know you're speaking in Building B, Room 10, on the campus of XYZ University in another state, ask what the room and building are like, if there are any special events that will be held prior to your talk or afterward, the history of the building and maybe even the history of the grounds. If the president of the United States once gave a talk in that very room, you might have just discovered a quick and funny opening that will endear you with the audience, especially if you can show some self-deprecating humor.

  - **DATE** – Researching historical events that occurred on the day of the talk is often a fascinating way to find anecdotal and informative material that will engage an audience early on, especially if you can present it as a story and tie it into the main messages. As an example, a little research showed me that ballroom dancing had been introduced on the same day (but many years earlier) the CEO I was working for at the time was speaking. Fortunately for me, he was speaking in a well-appointed ballroom of a nice hotel. Our key message was that the audience needed to embrace the Kyoto climate change treaty instead of fighting it. So we titled the talk Waltzing with Kyoto and alluded to dancing throughout the speech. It was a big hit!

  - **CURRENT EVENTS** – What will the audience members be discussing over coffee or tea during the meeting's break? The weather or politics? The

Super Bowl or the Olympics? It's worth a few minutes to pore through the newspaper and ensure you're up to date on the events the audience might be discussing.

- **POP CULTURE** – It's incredibly important to know the popular culture references of your audience. You already know—from your analysis—what the audience's age range and characteristics are. If you don't share those, find people who do and find out what's happening in their world of books, music, movies and TV.

Bucket Two: Body of Speech

This is the bread and butter of the speech you're writing, the content that could either tilt the audience in your favor or leave them flat and unresponsive. You'll want to conduct as specific research as you can here on your key arguments or key messages. You need to know what the primary issues are, what the audience believes about them and what others are saying about them. This is especially effective if you're writing a persuasive talk; it pays to know what you're up against. But even when the speech is more informational, it pays to list the points you want to make and begin gathering the evidence to support them. What kind of evidence? Look for:

- Statistics
- Anecdotes
- Quotations
- Testimony
- Stories
- Personal examples
- Humor

Bucket Three: Additional Support

With your key messages in hand, find the evidence and data to support them. You'll want to collect at least three or four points for each of your main arguments. The best supporting material is specific ... and varied. Some of this material may come to light as you're researching the main body of the speech. Set it aside, however, until you've actually written the talk. Then go back and insert the most useful information that supports your talk and main points. This makes better use of your time. You'll want to do research around categories such as these:

- **VISUALS** – Visuals aren't just important for electronic slide presentations. They can be useful, too, for pure speaking engagements. A speech on drunk driving to a group of teenagers, for example, might be more powerful if you bring in the twisted bumper from a wrecked car. But even traditional graphs and charts can be useful if they're big enough for the audience to see. (Visuals for electronic presentations are covered in a later chapter.)

- The best visuals are usually the most simple. Unusual visuals work well and are often memorable and helpful if you can introduce them early and reinforce them at the end. Veteran speechwriter Pete Weissman once showed an audience a tube and told them in his opening remarks that the tube held the one thing he would take from his office if he had to leave it in an emergency. He then left the tube on a table next to the podium and didn't reference it again, even as he closed his speech and opened up the talk for questions. One of the first questions, of course, was about the tube and he was able to use it to reinforce a key point in his speech in a humorous way. (Wondering what was inside the tube? It was a rubber chicken. He said it reminded him to, above all else, keep a sense of humor about life. Wise words for speechwriters everywhere.)

- **ANECDOTES** – Anecdotal information can be invaluable in breaking up your rhetoric with a small story or a reinforcing proof point. Anecdotes are often thought of as humorous, but serious anecdotes can work as well. Gen. Douglas MacArthur's famous Thayer Award speech at West Point began with an anecdote about the taxi driver who picked him up that morning. MacArthur was not only a student at West Point, but he became one of its most well-known commandants before he served in the Pacific theater during World War II. The morning of his speech, he stepped out of his hotel to hail a taxi for the ride to West Point where he would deliver his remarks. The doorman, hearing where the general wanted to go, said, "Wonderful place. Have you ever been there?" It was a wonderful anecdote that showed humility and humor in one swift blow.

You should also consider inserting anecdotes about:

- The location

- The topic

- Current events your audience would be familiar with

- The audience itself

- **HUMOR** – Humor can be an especially useful—and especially dangerous—tool to employ. It can be used early to warm up an audience or used later in the speech to wake them up between serious parts of the talk. Plus, shared humor can build a wonderful bond between speaker and audience. Humor works best when it:

- Is nonconfrontational

- Avoids politics/religion/race

- Is self-deprecating within limits

- Comes from someone else. This is particularly useful if your speaker is not naturally funny or adept at telling a story. A humorous quote from someone the audience already knows is funny, for example, can be substituted for homegrown humor. (Example: Mark Twain once pointed out that ...)

- Is organically connected to the speaker or the speech. Here's a good example: Boeing CEO Jim McNerney warmed up his audience of engineering students at the College of Engineering at the University of Michigan with the classic story of Icarus—with a twist. After telling of Daedalus' wings of feathers, fastened with linen and wax, he reminded them of how Icarus soared too close to the sun and melted the wax. "Though Icarus continued to flap his arms, they no longer caught the wind, and the poor boy plunged into the sea," McNerney said. "In the language of engineering, Icarus exceeded his thermal limits—leading to structural failure and a subsequent loss of control. Ladies and gentlemen, students and members of the faculty, that is the wonderful—but unforgiving—world of engineering!"

Humor can also be dangerous.

- Avoid traditional jokes—If you've heard it, the audience probably has, too.

- Never allow your speaker to make fun of his or her ability to speak, do research or be prepared. If the audience is going to spend 20 minutes or more listening to a speech, the last thing they want to hear is that the speaker just "threw the presentation together" on the plane or that he's not a good speaker. It's not what they expect from a leader. Speakers who make light of their own speaking abilities demonstrate an enormous lack of confidence and are extremely dispiriting.

- Humor won't work in every talk. There is no magic rule so you often have to let the subject matter be your guide. When in doubt, ask someone else to listen to the humor in context with the rest of the speech. BUT ... also consider how the humor may appear if it's taken out of context, an event which trips up even the seasoned speaker and writer. If in doubt, leave it out.

- **QUOTATIONS** – Many people don't like to use quotes because they feel self-conscious or believe the audience will think they're presenting material that's not their own. But a well-researched—and well-placed—quote can move your arguments forward quicker than any bit of logical reasoning by itself. The key is simply making sure the quote relates to the message.

- **SPECIAL CONCERNS** – Here's a speechwriting maxim: Audiences expect the truth. Any deviation in today's media-heavy, blog-filled world will be scrutinized in detail and your speaker's entire argument—and possibly their career—could be finished. In reality, there's no reason to fabricate or omit any facts in your speech or presentation. So here are a few things to consider as you're gathering and using research.

- **ATTRIBUTION** – Speeches aren't like term papers with footnotes and formal attributions. Still, it's always best to keep a record of where you found the information in your talk or presentation in case someone asks. Never mis-attribute information. (On the other hand, you can borrow credibility and enhance your speaker's character appeal by directly quoting or attributing material to a person the audience favors.)

- **OMISSION** – It never helps your argument to omit important points. Everyone expects you to stress your key messages. But you'll lose audience respect if you cite an opposition argument but leave out the most persuasive points. Audiences know a "straw man" when they see one.

- **EXAGGERATION** – Audiences today are sophisticated and quick. They'll know if you exaggerate a claim.

- **FABRICATION** – The worst sin of all for any speaker or writer—it's like lying on your resume. There's no need to make up statistics, quotes or even anecdotes. ✿

INSIDER TIP

#1 If you're speaking at a conference hotel, make friends with the concierge. That person can provide some of the most valuable, funny and interesting material you can work into a speech, even at the last minute. Ask them: What's the strangest request you've had? What's the hottest event/restaurant/tour being requested? What's the funniest thing you've seen in the lobby? Who was the most important figure to stay here recently? Not all will be accommodating but if you approach them when they're not busy and respect their knowledge and position, you can find interesting nuggets to drop in to your speech. And don't forget to tip them!

Humor with a Point

Humor is a great tool. It can make an audience feel at ease. It can lighten the mood. It can make a dull subject seem fresh and exciting. And, when it's self-effacing, it can show the speaker in a favorable light. But it can also teach a lesson.

The best humor—like the best anecdote and the best quote—has something to do with the subject at hand. In a sense, it's a proxy for the message. Why? Because sometimes, the humorous story is all the audience will remember. Here's a great example from William J. Bennett, the secretary of education under President Reagan. He has a tough task: talking about subjects like ethics and virtue. So how does he do it and not seem wooden, stiff and boring? Humor, of course.

> When I was secretary of education under President Reagan, I visited an elementary school in Raleigh, N.C. As I did at many of the 120 schools I visited during that period, I taught a lesson there on George Washington.
>
> Afterwards, I asked the kids if they had any questions, and one little guy raised his hand and asked, "Mr. Secretary, when you and President Reagan and the other people get together at meetings of the Cabinet, do you really eat Jelly Bellys?"
>
> He'd heard about Reagan's penchant for Jelly Belly jelly beans. I answered, "Yes, the president has a bowl of jelly beans at the meetings, and he eats some and passes them around, and I've had a few." And this kid looked me in the face and said, "I think you've had more than a few, Mr. Secretary."
>
> This was quite funny, and I remember President Reagan laughing when I told him about it. But the story also makes an important point. Do you recall when Gorbachev was visiting the U.S. and trying to figure out what America was like? He went walking up and down Connecticut Avenue, and he went over to the National Archives to look at documents. But he should have gone to that elementary school in Raleigh.
>
> I can guarantee you that never in the history of the Soviet Union did an 8-year-old look into the eyes of a heavyset minister of education and say, "I'll bet you eat all the caviar you can get your hands on."
>
> Maybe the kid's comment was a little fresh—a little over the top—but it showed that the ethos of liberty is in our hearts, and that is a good and important thing.
>
> Reprinted by permission from *Imprimis*, a publication of Hillsdale College.)

STEP 4:

Tell Me a Story

People are hungry for stories. It's part of our very being.

– Studs Terkel

How many times has this happened to you? On Monday morning, you walk into the office and someone asks a version of this question: "Did you do anything fun this weekend?"

Maybe you did and begin recounting your tale. And before you get to the end, several more people have gathered around to hear. These are hungry people.

Call it the Theory of the Campfire (or Theory of the Water Cooler, if you want a more modern twist) but the fact is that people love stories. There is something primordial—something deep in our psyches—that is attracted to them. It's why people are drawn to good books and movies. It's why they pick up the newspaper every day, watch the news on TV and hang around the water cooler. They love stories and they particularly love stories told by leaders.

Why? Because good stories told by leaders satisfy listeners on several levels. Stories are not only entertainment, they're informational. Most of them demonstrate a moral or learning and yet, they're not as overbearing as an order. In that way, leader stories convey an enormous amount of respect for the audience, respect that is incredibly appealing and more appreciated than a memo or email ever could be.

And yet, when it comes to sharing stories in a more formal setting—in a company meeting or from a podium—many leaders are reluctant. After all, shouldn't a well-thought-out and reasoned message be compelling enough? Shouldn't logic rule the day? Shouldn't any audience be swayed more by the hard cold purity of facts and data instead of the emotion?

The reality is that people are rarely influenced solely by data. People are faced with tons of data every day and ignore much of it. How many times have smokers heard about the dangers of cigarettes and yet don't stop smoking? Or the dangers of obesity and yet they continue to eat and fail to exercise? People react only so much to data and logic. What really influences them is when they get information that hits them where they think and where they feel. And you can only do that with stories.

I know you've heard this old saying: You can lead a horse to water, but you can't make it drink. Audiences are the same way. You can take them down a path of logic and data and lead them straight to the conclusion but you can't make them believe unless they want to.

Like horses, people are often stubborn, especially if it means giving up a position they've held for a long time or if it means amending their beliefs. So you have to allow them to make up their own minds. You must show them the respect of their being self-motivated, intelligent and careful thinkers. Stories are the perfect tool because they allow listeners to make sense of the data and reach their own conclusions.

Here's an example. Around the turn of this century, American businesses came under fire for their unethical behavior. The country had just witnessed several alarming episodes in corporate America, including the debacle at Enron where many of its leaders were questioned not just about their business practices but also their personal ethics. People were wondering aloud what caused businesses to conduct their business this way and the nation's prestigious business schools came under fire for failing to teach ethics.

Because of the uproar, leaders throughout the corporate world were recruited as speakers at MBA schools. Students needed to be instructed and the businesses—knowing a good PR opportunity when they saw one—were eager to oblige. But, what to say? The age-old question.

Some companies relied on logic and reason, showing the damage done by unethical companies. They presented slides with stock data and graphs showing consumer confidence while extolling the virtues of ethics. And they rolled out PowerPoint slides showing what their own company's ethics policy was.

Others took a different track, relying on stories to prove a point. One of those was Eastman Chemical Co., a large U.S. manufacturing firm founded by George Eastman in the 1920s to supply his parent company—Kodak—with chemicals and plastics he could no longer rely on getting from Europe.

When Eastman leaders hit the road to talk about ethics, they dug into their company history and pulled out a story from the early Kodak days. Kodak, after all, had a great brand and was synonymous with priceless memories. It was the company that allowed the common person to capture birthdays, anniversaries and vacations on film and save them for generations. The company had a reputation for quality film and, through very good marketing, a reputation that said it cared about its customers' lives. How many millions of people, faced with the choice of film brands at the corner drugstore, instinctively reached for the familiar yellow and red box instead of a competitor's simply because they had good feelings about Kodak? Who wouldn't, after all, want to capture their own "Kodak moment"?

Eastman piggybacked on the Kodak brand, so to speak, by telling a story about one of George Eastman's first ethical dilemmas. It was in the heyday of photography when photographers used large, cumbersome glass plates—instead of film—to record their images. George Eastman was just starting in the photography business but had established his new company as a quality supplier of these expensive glass plates. But it was still a struggling business. Profit margins were slim, and his customer base was mostly limited to the New York region. There wasn't much room for error. So you can imagine Mr. Eastman's distress when photographers began returning his glass plates and demanding refunds. Something in his process was wrong and photographers by the score were returning his product. Eastman faced a choice.

One option was to make good on the product and either refund the money or supply his customers with new plates. But that would be terribly expensive, possibly ruining him financially. The other option was to simply keep the proceeds, close his business in New York and move it somewhere else. Relocating might provide him time to repair his reputation before venturing into New York again. Then again, by staying and taking care of his customers, his reputation might swing the other way and he would have customers who kept coming back.

Needless to say, George Eastman stayed in New York. And, as he guessed, handing out refunds and new glass plates almost ruined him financially. But only for awhile. That act garnered him a tremendous amount of praise from his customers and helped solidify his reputation as a quality supplier.

Eastman Chemical used that story in numerous speeches over the years, softly hitching its own ethical wagon to that of its namesake. Now, it didn't hurt that the chemical company already had a solid reputation itself. It had won the coveted Malcolm Baldrige National Quality Award a few years earlier—the first major chemical company to achieve that honor—and had a history of philanthropy and community involvement. But its leaders also knew that simply running those factoids out in front of audiences would only go so far. What helped more than anything was telling a story that allowed the audience to make up its own mind about the company's ethics. The old adage—show, don't tell—was the key to the company making its case.

Only stories have that power because only stories convey the depth of emotion that audiences react to. They do that by allowing audience members to place themselves in the story, relate it to events in their own lives, and compare it to something personal to them. Every audience member listening to that story about George Eastman could identify with his dilemma. Every audience member has been in a similar circumstance as Eastman—perhaps not as dramatic but just as important on an individual basis—and faced his same choice. They knew what he *should* do and, when he did it, they transferred their warm feelings to the speaker.

The Benefits of Storytelling

Stories help speakers communicate in other ways, too. Here are a few examples of how stories aid:

1. **STORIES BRING THE MATERIAL TO LIFE** – If you ever had a boring, fact-based history teacher, you'll understand this instinctively. There are the facts and then there are the stories *behind* the facts. Stories allow abstract thoughts and data to become the concrete images, painted on the audience's mind. They provide context and help bring meaning to the material.

2. **STORIES LAST** – Let's say you meet someone at a party and share the customary information: where you were born, who you work for, and what school you attended. All facts and all subject to the vagaries of memory. The next day, you may

not remember any of it—except the funny story he told about the college room-mate. Stories remain in the mind far longer than the facts. Speechwriters can use that to their advantage by creating stories that linger in the audience's mind.

3. **STORIES GET PASSED ALONG** – Today they call it viral marketing. But the simple fact is that people not only like to hear stories, they like to tell stories. Picking stories that mean something to the individuals or the organization is a great way to get others to carry your message for you.

4. **STORIES ARE MORE BELIEVABLE** – Facts can be twisted. Data depends on interpretation. But stories have a built-in believability factor that's difficult to match. They have an aura of truth that's almost impossible to duplicate by simple reason and logic. Speakers can boost their own credibility simply through artful storytelling. There's an old Italian proverb that illustrates this: Tell me a fact and I'll learn. Tell me a truth and I'll believe. But tell me a story and it will live in my heart forever.

5. **STORIES HELP DEFINE HERITAGE** – Every company (and every individual for that matter) is an amalgam of the stories of their lives. On the negative side, how many companies—say Enron or Union Carbide, for instance—have their reputation destroyed or forever sullied by a story they prefer was never told? On the positive side, stories can allow speakers to mold the heritage and reputation of their own organizations. Stories about customer service, leadership, quality, honesty, charity, caring. These stories are present in every organization, just waiting for speechwriters to pull them out and use them. Tell enough of them and people will begin to model behavior accordingly because they begin to understand what's important to the organization. Stories define organizations by demonstrating what its leaders feel are worthy of repeating. It takes work and time to find these stories, but the payoff is tremendous.

6. **STORIES REACH ACROSS CULTURES, AGES AND ETHNIC DIVISIONS** – A good story is universal. After all, we've been telling them since we first learned to draw primitive figures on cave walls. Regardless of their cultural background or age, most listeners can put themselves or someone they know into the story and bridge the gap between the leader and the audience because stories involve people and, mostly, how they respond to situations. It's the ultimate tool to connect with your audience regardless of your varied backgrounds.

7. **STORIES ENTERTAIN** – People will listen (and listen longer) if you tell a story. The simple formula is: State a key point and tell a story, share some facts and then tell another story. By the time the speech is over, the audience may not even realize there was a speech. They'll think the speaker was entertaining.

8. **STORIES ENHANCE DELIVERY** – Regardless of how good (or bad) you might think your speaker is when delivering a talk in front of people, one

thing is certain: Their delivery is better when they're telling a story. How do I know? Because they've been doing it longer, they're more comfortable with the format and it seems more natural. Inserting stories into your speeches is an easy way to make your speaker a better communicator, get people to listen more intently and, frankly, let everyone have more fun.

The World is Full of Stories

There are lots of stories you can help your speakers tell. For the sake of simplicity, let's narrow them down to just three.

1. **WHO I AM** – This is probably the most important story your speaker will ever tell. Before people will trust your speaker, before they'll follow him, they need to know who he is. You can't do that with resume-like data. You have to show through stories about his life and his experiences. Sometimes those are very personal stories about how he grew up or how he worked his way through college. They might be about a personal crisis in his life that profoundly changed his outlook. It might be a story about a childhood friend or simply a funny-thing-happened-on-the-way-over-here story. Then again, it doesn't have to be a personal story at all. It just has to be a story that reveals the speaker somehow, even if it's about someone else. And if your speaker genuinely likes to tell humorous stories and is good at it, then go with that as well. After all, the subject—and how well it's related—can tell the audience something about the speaker, and telling funny stories shows the audience the speaker likes to laugh, has a good sense of humor and won't be boring. For years I've spoken at communication conferences, retelling the same story about a funny incident involving my oldest son when he was 4 years old. He's 15 now but I still tell the story because I find humor helps break the ice, it tells the audience that I'm a family man and it relates back to the main point I'm trying to make. I could just as easily tell a fable, a historical story or even a parable from the Bible. Each would send a message about who I am and what I believe is important.

2. **WHY I'M HERE** – Another powerful type of story, especially for leaders. "Why I'm Here" stories are, in fact, absolutely necessary for many leaders. Not all, but many. For leaders who come into organizations undergoing difficult times, these types of stories are crucial. They need to convey their true purpose, the only way leaders can enlist the help of others. Of course, the "Why I'm Here" story can be just as effective for those leaders who are speaking on behalf of not-for-profit or community groups. A story about the personal philosophy that has guided the speaker to a particular cause can be extremely powerful. People want to know the "why" just as much as the "who." This is not a time to hide your speaker's passion. Drag it out, share it and you'll be amazed at how many people will respond positively.

3. **TEACHING STORIES** – There are a variety of stories leaders can use in teaching others. Stories are useful in helping others know what to do, how to do it and what behaviors are appropriate in the organization. In a sense, they're like a map for listeners who know that, if they pay attention and model their behavior, they'll find a chest full of treasure. If there's a customer service problem in your organization, for example, a story about how one employee successfully solved the crisis and what that accomplished for the company is ideal. It's much better than merely presenting trend data on customer complaints or the number of product returns. Why? Because it presents a problem *and* a solution, a hallmark of good leadership. Other kinds of teaching stories include the inspirational story, the values-in-action story, the cautionary tale and the story of personal determination and perseverance. Each has its place in the speechwriter's toolbox. Each can be used as a way to connect with the audience on a personal level, involve them in the speaker's world and engage them in a larger mission.

Where to Find Stories

Sometimes good stories come to you naturally. Other times, finding just the right story takes a structured effort. Here are a few places where you can actively look for stories to put into your talk or to simply file away for a future talk.

1. **CUSTOMER LETTERS** – Organizations usually get far more letters than they can ever respond to. In larger Fortune 500 companies, there are entire departments where customer letters are handled. This is a great place to find stories to illustrate values-in-action or to reinforce the "what our organization is about" talk. But smaller organizations, too, get letters and they're an excellent source for your talk. They add credibility and variety as well as emotion. Ask around. Do some probing. Engage the sales team and customer service groups. You'll be amazed at what people will tell you.

2. **ORGANIZATIONAL HISTORY** – The organization you're writing for—or even about—has some kind of history and it's probably a good one. How it was founded. How it overcame obstacles. How it persevered when others failed. A little digging—which often means talking to retirees and librarians and rummaging through newspapers—can yield wonderful, inspirational stories that can make an audience swell in admiration.

3. **PERSONAL STORIES** – These are your speaker's personal triumphs and, occasionally, failures. Either way, they all combined to create a leader and are worthy of a story. If—and this is a big if—the lesson is imitable by the audience. There has to be an "if I can do it so can you" ending to personal stories or they end up sounding self-serving and arrogant. Failures, in particular, are great stories that can show humility and reinforce that the speaker has

learned his lessons the hard way. In fact, there's nothing an audience loves to hear more than how a speaker has suffered … and overcome.

4. **BIOGRAPHIES** – Does your speaker have a personal hero? Maybe a favorite business leader or community servant? Have you asked? If so, the stories can be valuable in two ways: They show the audience who the speaker is and what he or she admires while also lending themselves as message support and entertainment. Plus, it's an easy way to borrow credibility, especially if you're certain the audience admires the same hero, too. Some of these people we admire already have books and magazine articles written about them, full of stories you can borrow. But the person doesn't have to be anyone famous. It could be the pastor from the speaker's church or a co-worker who volunteers for a local charity. It could be a family member or mentor who taught a valuable lesson. The point is that the stories of those who inspire the speaker can inspire others as well and can help demonstrate the "Who I Am" message.

5. **FABLES, MOVIES AND BOOKS** – Audiences are often comforted to hear a familiar story adapted to a contemporary problem. Most fables and folk tales have a moral which can be easily tailored for your use. Why not use the *Wizard of Oz* in an inspirational message about finding your bliss? Or perhaps the story of Job as a cautionary tale about losing faith? Popular movies and books are especially useful and can be reused to great effect. The best thing is that the audience is familiar with them and, once they recognize that they also know the story, will begin nodding their heads. It might be subtle, but it's a sign of acceptance and a sign the speaker is connecting.

How to Use Stories

There are lots of ways to use stories, but only a few ways to use them effectively. The best places are at the beginning and in the middle of a speech. Stories at the beginning are a great way to frame the entire subject and set the right tone. A tale about a beleaguered employee who went out of the way to help a longtime customer is a wonderful way to begin a talk about service. Relating how a child's innocence helped the speaker see "the bigger truth" in a situation, told at the beginning of a talk, can galvanize an audience by showing humility and warmth.

If you choose to use a story at the beginning, a great technique is to simply begin by telling the story. Don't write "Hello, it's nice to be here" or any other introductory remarks. Simply start by telling the story. It's astounding how rapt and attentive an audience can become if you do this. You'll have their attention, which is sometimes the hardest part. If you need to come back and thank the host organization, that's fine. By then, you'll already have the audience's attention.

Stories told in the middle of a talk are most often used to support one of your key messages. But they have the added bonus of being able to add humor and levity and to break up what could otherwise be a particularly long and boring section. Just remember that the further into a talk you go, the shorter the story should be. If you've already told the audience that you have three points to make and you've shared two of those points with them, they will have subconsciously concluded that you're two-thirds through your talk. If you suddenly begin telling a lengthy story on point No. 3, they may feel restless and resentful. You can tell, because audiences that feel like you've worn out your welcome will start straightening their papers, checking their watches or squirming in their seats. Unless, of course, it's a great story, which brings me to the final point about stories: They must be good, appropriate stories.

So what makes a good story? The same thing that makes a good book or a good movie: a compelling beginning, followed by a crisis or key event, a resolution and, for our purposes, a moral. The beginning must, in fact, start off by capturing the audience's imagination, so borrow a technique from the movies by skipping the introductory material and beginning, the story as close to the action as possible.

The crisis or key event, of course, relates to the main message, however tenuously. You must be able to describe the problem in a way the audience can understand and relate to. In other words, they should be able to say to themselves, "Yeah, I've been there."

The ending should show the resolution and what was learned. It should be short and to the point. While the story doesn't have to be funny—although humor is a great way to connect with the audience—consider the ending of the story to be the punch line of a joke.

Finally, like any good movie or book, good stories are full of descriptions and suspense. Details make a story come alive for the listener, allow them to be part of the story, and fire their imagination. And suspense creates a nice bit of tension with the audience that's fun for them and you.

This isn't the time to hold back. If you want to be heard and understood, you need to be a bold storyteller. ☼

INSIDER TIPS

#1 Stories are more effective at the beginning and middle of your talk. Audiences are more receptive to them early. As the talk progresses, and the audience begins subconsciously calculating the amount of time until you finish speaking, you don't want to distract them with a story they might think will prolong the talk.

#2 Make sure you have the permission of the characters in your story before including them in your talk. What may seem like an innocent or even appreciative mention may not be welcomed by those highlighted.

SPEECH EXCERPT

The Canadian Economy

A speech comparing the Canadian and American economies sounds boring, doesn't it? Not in the capable hands of Mark Steyn. A writer himself, Steyn was once asked to give a speech at Hillsdale College comparing America's economic model with that of his native Canada.

Steyn isn't your ordinary presenter, however. It's obvious early on that he's a storyteller, too. In this excerpt, he's already told the audience there are five main differences between the two economies. This is how he describes difference No. 3:

The third difference is that Canada's economy is more subsidized. Almost every activity amounts to taking government money in some form or other. I was at the Summit of the Americas held in Canada in the summer of 2001, with President Bush and the presidents and prime ministers from Latin America and the Caribbean. And, naturally, it attracted the usual antiglobalization anarchists who wandered through town lobbing bricks at any McDonald's or Nike outlet that hadn't taken the precaution of boarding up its windows. At one point I was standing inside the perimeter fence sniffing tear gas and enjoying the mob chanting against the government from the other side of the wire, when a riot cop suddenly grabbed me and yanked me backwards, and a nanosecond later a chunk of concrete landed precisely where I had been standing. I bleated the usual "Oh my God, I could have been killed" for a few minutes and then I went to have a café au lait. And while reading the paper over my coffee, I learned that not only had Canadian colleges given their students time off to come to the summit to riot, but that the Canadian government had given them $300,000 to pay for their travel and expenses. It was a government-funded antigovernment riot! At that point I started bleating, "Oh my God, I could have been killed at taxpayer expense." Say what you like about the American trust-fund babies who had swarmed into demonstrate from Boston and New York, but at least they were there on their own dime. Canada will and does subsidize anything.

Reprinted by permission from *Imprimis*, a publication of Hillsdale College.)

To Show or Tell:
When to Use PowerPoint

The newest computer can merely compound, at speed, the oldest problem
in the relations between human beings, and in the end the communicator will be
confronted with the old problem, of what to say and how to say it.

– Edward R. Murrow

Edward R. Murrow, the famous architect of the early CBS News staff, knew perhaps more than anyone the power of the spoken word and the power of the visual. He began his professional career, after all, in radio, where the only way to communicate was through words, carefully chosen, to paint a picture in the audience's mind.

Later, of course, Murrow was able to physically combine words and pictures when he moved over to television. It was a technology he seemed to have many reservations about but still used as well as any newsman of his day. He understood the influence visuals provided to move people when words could not. But, as most good news people do today, he never forgot that it's difficult to pass along the heavy stuff—understanding and realization—with words alone. It was Murrow who said, "Just once in a while let us exalt the importance of ideas and information."

Today, Murrow's battle goes on, and we still face his challenge of "what to say and how to say it." Should you show ... or tell? For a lot of speechwriters, it boils down to this: Use PowerPoint or another computer-based presentation system ... or write a traditional speech?

Unfortunately, making this decision isn't even an issue for many people today. Especially for those working in corporate America, there is an unconscious bias for showing through the use of computer-built presentations. Everyone from the silver-haired CEO in the corner office to the newly minted MBA grad has somehow come to believe that charts and slides showing financial information and market share is enough to persuade audiences. In fact, many corporate people actually *think* in PowerPoint and you'll hear things like: "How many slides do you think this will take?" or "I want to do this presentation in no more than 10 slides."

As a result, PowerPoint becomes their master and, often, their only muse. PowerPoint presentations, in other words, run amok in the business world because most of these

47

leaders have never been told that data alone is rarely the key factor in creating under-standing or eliciting action.

As a speechwriter, however, you should make a conscious decision not only about what to say, but how to say it. Should you show (with PowerPoint)? Or should you tell (with words)? Forget what everyone else is doing, and make your decision based on what's right for your audience and your message. There are times when PowerPoint is absolutely the right choice just as there are more times when it is absolutely the wrong choice. Knowing when and why can make a huge difference in whether your speaker is heard and understood.

The smart speechwriter will work backwards from the desired conclusion and develop a talk or presentation that supports the goal. Therefore, using a formal speech or talk versus a computer presentation such as PowerPoint should be determined by the *type* of talk you're giving and what you want to *accomplish*. The truth is that different formats have different attributes and send vastly different signals to the audience.

In general, the lower down on the communication hierarchy you're targeting, the eas-ier it is to use PowerPoint. The higher you target, the more you need face-to-face, spoken communication without PowerPoint.

Rule of thumb for PowerPoint advantage vs. talk:

Type of Speech	Traditional Speech	Electronic Presentation
Informative		◎
Creating Understanding		◎
Reinforcing Values	◎	
Changing Attitudes	◎	
Eliciting Action	◎	

In the end, each format has advantages and disadvantages you need to consider, depend-ing on what you want to accomplish. Let's look at each type of speech and discuss the relative strengths of show vs. tell.

Informative Speech

The idea here is simply to pass along information and, often, PowerPoint works very well. The printed word on the screen gives people time to read the material themselves and digest it at their own speed. It's easier, in other words, to follow along and absorb large amounts of the Who, What, When and Where type of information.

PowerPoint has the advantage here, too, of assuring that different audiences hear the same messages. If the idea is to present the same information to several different groups (or if you have other speakers who need to deliver the same information to different groups), you'll find great comfort in knowing that they are all singing from the same hymnal, so to speak.

The slides in PowerPoint are easy to update so if you have to present the same information every month or quarter, this is the way to go. You can update the material on the fly and incorporate new data with ease.

Financial data—with charts and graphs—lend themselves to PowerPoint with exceptional ease. It's one thing to say that fundraising efforts have fallen by 50 percent in the last six months; it's another to see the steep downward slope on a graph.

Other types of presentations that lend themselves to PowerPoint include: organizational charts, safety updates, project updates that include various team members, and anything that requires pictures (such as car accidents, building updates, storm damage).

Some caveats, however. Remember that you will be heavily dependent on technology that may not cooperate on any given day. You'll have to ensure that the room you plan to present in has the capability to use PowerPoint and is lit accordingly (dim lighting—but not dark). Plus, you'll have to carry the PowerPoint with you some way. That's fairly easy to do with the small portable memory sticks available now. Just be forewarned that those, too, can fail. And often at just the wrong time.

If you use PowerPoint for one of these presentations, it's often a good idea to also bring along handouts that the audience can take away AFTER the presentation. (Distributing handouts before the talk literally invites people to ignore the speaker.) Handouts can reinforce the message being delivered and reinforce your speaker as a provider of information.

Can these informative talks be done without PowerPoint? Absolutely, especially if the message is short. Generous pay raises for everyone? Skip the PowerPoint and allow them to see you delivering that news directly. It will only reinforce goodwill. The same goes for changes in leadership and other brief announcements.

Creating Understanding

This is a tough one but, in general, the advantage goes slightly to PowerPoint. You're often showing why a decision was made or how it was reached. Sometimes, that decision is data driven and it's useful to share that same information with the audience. You can walk the audience through the same decision-making steps, creating understanding as you go along.

Just remember: Credibility is important here. The audience not only needs to understand the data, they need to believe the presenter. That's why it's often good to use PowerPoint here as a guide and not as the entire presentation. The fact is that you need people looking at the speaker as also the leader at this communication level and every level above. They need to see the leader's eyes and they need to see the leader's body language so they can judge for themselves—absent of the PowerPoint data—what *the leader* believes.

One good way to do that is to reserve PowerPoint for the middle of the talk. Speak for several minutes to establish credibility, use PowerPoint to share data, and then close without the PowerPoint when the audience is forced to turn their eyes back to the speaker. Slides are cold and passive; leaders should be warm and engaging. Use that to your advantage if your goal is to create understanding.

Reinforcing Shared Values – Changing Attitudes – Eliciting Action

Every level from here up on the five-step communication hierarchy is best served by the personal and direct appeal that can only be delivered by a person. Why? Because success on every level here depends most heavily on emotion. Yes, logic is important. But unless the audience members believe the speaker/leader, they'll never be won over.

PowerPoint simply can't deliver an emotional appeal because, more than anything, it directs eyes away from the leader/speaker who is, after all, the real source of power and influence.

That's not to say that you can never use PowerPoint in a talk designed to elicit action or change behaviors. Speakers can often use video embedded in a PowerPoint presentation, for example, to great effect, even in a persuasive talk. If you do, however, it should be short and reinforcing. It should never be the entire presentation or even the majority. If you use it for one of these talks, limit its use to no more than 20 percent, preferably near the beginning.

If you are using a video—a television commercial or ad, for example—one good technique is to open the presentation with it. If the speech is in front of a large crowd, beginning with a video before the speaker even gets onstage is often an exciting way to start because of its wow factor, especially if the commercial is funny or well-admired. It's yet another way to enhance credibility—this time from something that is already audience-approved.

The main takeaway is that—as a leader—your speaker should never decide how to present simply on the basis of what others have done. Work backward from what you want to do and then decide on whether you want to show, tell, or show and tell.

Being a contrarian—simply talking in front of people when others rely on Power-Point—can be a huge advantage. Your speaker will seem warmer and more personable. People will feel the speaker is more open and approachable, increasing the chances they will ask questions. And it will increase the chances to begin a dialogue with the audience because they will see the speaker's passion and mastery of the material as all positives and will become engaged themselves. That's what real leaders do—they engage people and enlarge their opportunities.

Here are some quick advantages and disadvantages of PowerPoint vs. talking. Decide for yourself how you want to be seen and heard:

PowerPoint

ADVANTAGES

* Easy to look "professional."

* Can easily incorporate other types of audiovisual material.

* The presenter can easily insert slides from one presentation to another.

* Can make the presenter feel more secure because eyes are not on him or her all the time.

DISADVANTAGES

- Fosters passive learning by relying on a "receiving only" format.

- Heavily dependent on technology—greater chance that technical problems will disrupt the presentation.

- Complex or large slide decks are often difficult to physically transfer.

- Effective use of backgrounds, font sizes, images are often ignored.

- Often forces the reader to ignore the speaker's words in favor of reading material on screen.

- Does not lend itself to rhetorical techniques that make talks and presentations more enjoyable, easier to digest and more effective.

- Because presenters are often looking at the slides, too, it stifles the feedback they might otherwise get by looking directly at members of the audience and seeing their body language. Therefore, it makes adjusting the message "on the fly" difficult.

- De-emphasizes the speaker and the speaker's credibility, two important ingredients to a successful presentation.

Speech or talk

ADVANTAGES

- Puts a premium on the speaker and speaker's credibility.

- Allows greater use of stories and traditional rhetorical devices that move a speech forward.

- Allows the presenter to watch the audience, determine mood and adjust accordingly.

- Can be adapted easily from audience to audience.

- Not dependent on high technology.

- Warmer and more personable.

- Can easily make and send copies of the talk to others.

- Allows the speechwriter to easily craft preapproved quotes that can be used by the media and others.

- Protects the speaker when quotes are used because the speech provides a record of what was said and the context in which the quotes were presented.

- Easily portable from location to location.

- Allows the speaker to provide something fresh and different from the PowerPoint presenters.

- Easy to leverage into other formats and uses such as in news releases, op-ed pieces, etc.

DISADVANTAGES

- Sometimes seen as "old school."

- Requires practice to be good.

- More difficult to show detailed information like financial graphs and charts.

- Can make the speaker more nervous because there is no slide deck to hide behind.

- More difficult—but not impossible—to incorporate audio or video material. ☼

INSIDER TIPS

#1 Regardless of whether your presentation is captured in a PowerPoint slide deck or written down on paper, back it up. Have multiple copies with you. And, if you're traveling from one city to the next, save the copies in separate locations. If your suitcase carrying one copy is lost by the airline, you'll still have a backup in your carry-on luggage or briefcase.

STEP 6

Sign, Sign, Everywhere a Sign: How to Lead Your Audience

Nothing is so simple that it cannot be misunderstood.

- Freeman Teague, Jr.

In its most simple form, the ability to write and deliver effective speeches is about sending a message to somebody else with as little misunderstanding as possible.

If you say, "The project deadline is Thursday," for example, people should hear and understand that "the project deadline is Thursday."

Of course, communication is really never that simple. For various reasons, people hear different things. Some may hear that the deadline is Tuesday instead of Thursday. Some may hear Thursday but think you surely meant *next* Thursday. Others may hear exactly what you said but not realize you meant *their* project.

Thursday comes and goes and no one turns in the project work. "What happened?" you ask. "How simple do I have to make it?"

There are two problems that are best shown in the simple diagram below, adapted from the classic Shannon-Weaver model of communication.

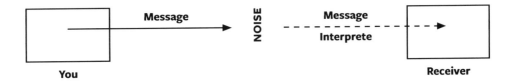

The first problem is that, between the message and the receiver, there is noise. The second is that the receiver has to redefine the message, based on that noise.

In this instance, noise can be anything. It could literally be noise between the speaker and the listener—a jackhammer outside the meeting room or a cellphone ringing. It could be feedback in the sound system or someone talking loudly at the next table and drowning out the speaker's voice.

But noise can take many forms. For example, noise could be added because the speaker and listener have different cultural references and beliefs. It could be as simple as a

50-year-old executive trying to speak to a group of teenagers; they won't share the same set of cultural backgrounds of music, arts or even pop culture. But it could also be an American speaker addressing a foreign audience; there will be language barriers as well as barriers that come from having different values and cultures.

Noise can also be spatial in its origin. Perhaps the presentation was delivered in a PowerPoint presentation and someone sitting in the back couldn't see the small type. You inadvertently introduced noise into the communication process and interrupted the ability of the audience to properly interpret the message. Another type of noise? Body language. When the body language doesn't match the speaker's words, it creates noise that changes the message. The classic example is the presidential debate between Richard Nixon and John F. Kennedy. On television, Nixon's nervous body language didn't match his confident words. The result was that people watching the debate on television had a different reaction from those who listened to it on the radio.

In its most basic form, noise is anything that degrades the information or changes the meaning of the message from when it leaves the speaker's lips until it reaches the listener's brain. We say one thing. But because of a variety of different noises (attitudes, beliefs, inappropriate body language, etc.), the message gets degraded and reinterpreted.

Part of your job as a speechwriter is to craft a speech and an event that eliminates as much of that noise as possible so the message your audience hears is the one you intended to send. Everything must support the message and, if possible, amplify it.

How to do that? There are a variety of ways and we've covered some of them early on when you did your audience research. Simply understanding your audience—its likes and dislikes, cultural references and beliefs—can dramatically reduce some of the noise.

Making sure your PowerPoint is legible and easy to follow is another. (That will be covered more in Step 8.)

One of the most important ways, though, is how you structure the speech. Structure is immensely important because it gives your talk a framework that allows the audience to follow along. Think of it this way: Imagine loading up all of your listeners in a large truck, blindfolding them and telling them something like: "We're going to take a trip now. I'm not going to tell you where we're going, you won't be able to look out of the window to judge for yourself, but when I stop the truck, you'll know we've arrived. And by the way, I'm going to tell you a story as we travel."

They wouldn't be very comfortable, would they? And they probably wouldn't listen to the story, no matter how good it was.

Listeners need structure just as travelers need road signs. Knowing where the speaker intends to take them reduces noise and allows their brain to focus on the message instead of the trip.

Here's a great example of someone who gives his audience a sign about where he intends to take them.

A few years ago, Michael Dell of Dell computers made remarks at the Center for Strategic and International Studies. After his brief introductory remarks, he stated his key message:

> There has never been a time in the history of business where it is more important for organizations of all sizes and types to partner together to positively impact the Earth we all share.

That's the biggest sign because he's told them where he's going. But, he's not finished. He gives them two landmarks to look for along the way:

> I just left a meeting of the Technology CEO Council, a group of eight CEOs in the tech sector. Each company is pursuing the energy issue in its own way. They're all focused on how they can be more energy-efficient and minimize their impact on the environment. And, of course, the White House is hosting the Climate Change conference this week to discuss this very issue.
>
> As a global technology leader, we meet with customers and policymakers from around the world on a regular basis. Through these conversations two things are clear:
>
> First, it's not enough that Dell just be an environmental leader—we must also partner with our customers through the technology we deliver to dramatically improve their environmental performance.
>
> Second, these efforts are shaped by The ReGeneration. The term "ReGeneration" refers to people of all ages who share a common interest in renewable resources, recycling and other ways of sustaining the earth's natural environment.

Dell's use of "... through these conversations, two things are clear ..." is a sign that he's going to build his talk around these two areas. One. Two. The simplest of structures audiences can follow. Think of them as noise reducers.

You build these noise reducers into the remarks you write by the structure you choose. And, yes, every talk you write must have a structure. Just like every story has a Beginning, Middle and End, every speech must have an Opening, the Body and a Close. We'll cover what to put into each of these sections in Step 7: Writing. But before you can write your remarks down, you need to choose a structure that will reduce noise and help the audience follow the speech.

How to Select a Structure

The secret to a good speech structure is developing one the audience can follow. It's as simple as that. In fact, you already use structures every day when talking with people. One of the most common structures is the one people use when they're telling stories about themselves and what they've done or accomplished. It's a chronological structure built around a time sequence. It's probably the most comfortable structure but hardly the only one. Here are some of the most used structures that may fit your speaker's style and talks.

Chronological

This is among the most common structures useful for leaders who have to deliver an Informative talk. Imagine, for example, writing a speech that would tell a group of employees about the company's decision to change office buildings. If it's noncontroversial and the "why" is easily explainable, the main questions for your audience will be: What do I need to do and when? A time-based talk, giving a clear chronological order of events, would be extremely helpful to your audience. Dates become signposts the audience can follow.

Spatial or Geographic

This type of structure, like the time-based, is often very good for informative talks. Instead of time, it groups topic areas by their spatial relationship to one another such as top to bottom, right to left.

A leader sharing a company's sales revenue for the year, for example, might divide the data into geographic sets of Northeast, Southeast, Southwest, Midwest, West. It's best used, of course, when the geographic divisions make sense. In the example above, if the same company had relatively few sales west of the Mississippi, for instance, the sales leader might group his talk around Northeast, Southeast and West.

This structure works well for discussing broad categories that are already grouped. For instance, when discussing an organization's priorities, you could easily group them as Most Important, Moderately Important, Least Important.

Topical

Topical structures can be powerful because they allow speakers to talk around a set of related ideas. One idea supports the others and, most importantly, an overall thesis. The trick is to introduce the ideas early and remind the audience of where you are in the speech.

This is one of the best structures to use when you are trying to persuade or elicit action. You make a statement or claim—your thesis—and then give the proof why the statement is true. Here's an example of a topical structure used by Microsoft Chairman Bill Gates when he spoke at the World Economic Forum in Davos, Switzerland, in 2008:

> **MAIN STATEMENT:** Billions of people who need the great inventions of the computer age have no way of expressing their need to the market. If we are going to have a chance of changing their lives, we need not just technology innovation, but a system innovation.

> **TOPICAL POINT 1:** Creative capitalism can provide for people's needs because of its ability to make self-interest serve the wider interest.

> **TOPICAL POINT 2:** To harness the power of creative capitalism, it should have two missions: making profits and improving the lives of those who don't fully benefit from today's market forces.

TOPICAL POINT 3: There is a growing understanding around the world that when change is driven by proper incentives, you have a sustainable plan for change, because profits and recognition are renewable resources.

Elimination (or Compare and Contrast)

By removing, one by one, all of the alternatives to an argument, a speaker can successfully make a persuasive argument. This is a great structure when the speaker and the audience already share the same values and agree on the issue. In other words, it's best used at the top of the five-step communication hierarchy: Changing Behaviors and Eliciting Action. By comparing his preferred alternatives to the nonpreferred, a speaker can often get agreement and understanding on moving forward.

Pro-Con

Another useful structure, the Pro-Con outline allows a speaker to show the relative merits of a course of action. Again, this is most useful near the top of the communication hierarchy.

Numbered Lists

A very simple—but also tremendously effective—way to organize a talk. It's as simple as saying, "The three most important ideas I want to share with you are ..." Lists serve as natural signs for the audience (especially those taking notes) and is probably the most used and most powerful structure you can use. It's the one I use most often because of its simplicity and effectiveness. The best way to use this is by 1) stating the problem; 2) stating your thesis; 3) providing your numbered solution; 4) following through by clearly stating when you transition between points; and 5) close by restating your thesis and numbered points.

Other Structures

Although not as common as the ones described above, there are a variety of other patterns you can build a speech around. Each provides its own particular signs and can act as noise reducers when used with the appropriate audience.

CAUSE-EFFECT – Useful for explaining the "what" but rarely the "why" of a situation. Reserve this for Informative talks.

PROBLEM-SOLUTION-OUTCOME – An effective way to help audiences see the path forward, especially if you provide the outcome. Showing the benefits of implementing a solution is a requirement for speakers so make sure you follow through on this three-part pattern.

SPORTS ANALOGY – Depending on the audience, this can be a fun and creative way to build a talk while also being entertaining. If you're writing a speech on quality initiatives at a golf resort, why not structure it around ways to shave strokes off your quality game. Comparing your progress against goals using a baseball analogy ("we're rounding third and heading for home!") might be fun for your audience. The key to success using these types of structure is to make sure the audience is the right age and gender to appreciate the reference.

FAIRY TALES – Every culture has its own set of fairy tales and folk stories. In the U.S., for example, nearly everyone knows Goldilocks and the Three Bears and Jack and the Beanstalk. You can build a theme around these tales and have fun in the process.

Remember, no one will follow the speaker blindly into the forest, even if he or she is a great leader. Structure the talk so leaders know where they're going. Give them easily identifiable signs to let them know they're still on the right path. Make it easy for them to follow along, reduce the noise as much as possible, and, above all, have fun. ✿

INSIDER TIPS

#1 You can often combine structures to great effect. If you're using a Problem-Solution pattern, inserting a short List to help expand on a point, can be an extremely useful way to help your audience follow along.

#2 Fairy tales and folk stories are often effective when your speaker addresses a foreign crowd. Talk with people on the ground, find a well-known folk tale the audience will be familiar with and build a thesis around it. It will not only resonate with the audience, it will show your speaker respects the culture.

STEP 7:

More Structure and (finally!) Words

Every writer I know has trouble writing.

– Joseph Heller, author, *Catch-22*

If you talk to enough speechwriters you begin to understand that, in some ways, *writing* the speech is a bit over-rated. Sure, you're probably a good writer or you wouldn't have the job. But ... the truth is that writing is only part of a speechwriter's job and, ironically (especially given that "writer" is in the job title) only a small part of the job.

The majority of what a speechwriter really does is figure out how to say what needs to be said. It's not enough to have the right words; you also have to have them in the right order for the right reasons. Which is why—before you really start writing—you need to consider how the various parts of the speech fit together. A simple and traditional speech structure, for example, has three parts—the Opening, the Body and the Close. Each part is distinct and important in its own right and deserves some thought about how you can use them to ensure the words you do eventually put onto paper work for the audience. Plus, by carving the speech up into sections, it makes the actual writing job that much easier. What could be a 6,000-word mega-writing project, can be broken into manageable parts.

Besides, if you've already prepared the key messages and developed the main structure, the actual writing should be easy. You've done the hard work; now all you have to do is put the pieces together to form a whole talk—a talk that doesn't sound like bits and pieces but an entire address that's effective for your speaker and the audience.

In this chapter, I'll give you two different ways to organize a speech. The traditional simplified version is the one mentioned above: Open, Body and Close. But I'll also share with you a different, more detailed model called Monroe's Motivated Sequence. They are similar and which one you use depends on preference.

A word to the wise is in order before you start, however: This is not the time to agonize over specific word choices or even phrasing. If a good phrase comes to mind, by all means capture it. But the polishing and cleaning up will come next. The object here is to simply get started by putting words on paper.

The Simple Structure: Opening, Body and Close

This structure works so well because everyone is familiar with it. It's the same structure used in folk tales, magazine stories and novels. It's the same one we use over the water cooler on Monday mornings. It's easy to imagine and even easier to put into practice because just as every story has a Beginning, Middle and End, every talk has an Opening, Body and Close.

The Opening

The Opening of your talk should take no more than 10 to 15 percent of your total speaking time. During that time, you have to do four things very quickly to ensure the audience will stay with your speaker through the main portion of your talk. You must convey to the audience that the speaker:

1. Cares;

2. Understands the audience's issues;

3. Is the right person to address those issues;

4. Is warm and personable (even if he isn't).

Here's a great example from actor Alan Alda, who gave the 1980 commencement address at Connecticut College. Notice how he accomplishes each of the four critical parts of the Opening.

> I'm here today for a very special reason.
>
> When my daughter, Eve, was small, every dinner conversation would go roughly the same way. I would introduce a fascinating topic. Then I would make some glittering comments and generally attack it from all sides until Eve or one of her sisters would indicate a sufficiently low level of interest to make me grind to a stuttering halt.
>
> ### *Stories of children show his warmth.*
>
> "Now Eve is graduating college, and I've been asked by her class if I would give a little talk. Of course I accepted. This will be the first time in 21 years that she'll listen to one of my speeches all the way through.
>
> ### *His acceptance of this personal invitation to speak shows he's caring. The joke shows he's personable.*
>
> As I stand here, I'm probably experiencing what most parents feel today: a desire, a little inner tug, to say something that will count in a special way.
>
> ### *By sharing his unease, he confirms that he understands the issue.*
>
> Deep in our hearts we know that the best things said come last. People will talk for hours saying nothing much and then linger at the door with

words that come with a rush from the heart. Doorways, it seems, are where the truth is told. We are all gathered at a doorway today. It's the end of something and the beginning of something else. And my guess is there will be a lot of lingering at the door today with the hope that one of us will say something that will somehow express what can't be said in words.

We linger there with our hand on the knob chattering away like Polonius to Laertes. Now remember, "Neither a borrower nor a lender be," and don't forget, "This above all: To thine own self be true and it must follow, as the night the day, thou canst not then be false to any man." But the very best things said often slip out completely unheralded and preceded by the words, "Oh, by the way."

I hear that patients will talk to their therapists for an hour, hardly saying anything, and just as they're leaving, turn at the door and say, "Oh, by the way," and in one sentence reveal everything they've been avoiding for 50 minutes.

In real life, when Polonius had finished giving all that fatherly advice to his son, who probably wasn't paying all that much attention anyway, he must have said, just as the boy was stepping into his boat, "Oh, by the way, if you get into trouble, don't forget you can always call me at the office."

As we stand in the doorway today, these are my parting words to my daughter, Eve. I may sound a little like Polonius, Eve, but Polonius and I have something in common. Like all fathers, we love to hear ourselves talk. And there are so many things I want to tell you.

> *His observations of life demonstrate he's the right person to address the issues of the day.*

How to show the speaker:

1. Cares

    *   **THROUGH RESEARCH** – A great way to show the speaker cares about the audience and the issues is by dropping in bits of history about the institution, the location or the people involved. It demonstrates that the speaker cared enough to ask questions and learn more.

    *   **BRIEF STORY** – Stories that show your speaker's relationship to the issues allow him or her to show a caring side that may otherwise be difficult to convey.

    *   **CREATIVITY** – Opening with something creative—a poem, a letter the speaker or the organization received or even a song—shows that the speaker is going the extra mile for the audience.

2. Understands

- **RHETORICAL QUESTIONS** – At the beginning, rhetorical questions can be an effective way to arrest the audience's attention. Notice how Peter Hain, a member of the British Parliament, forgoes the traditional "I'm glad to be here" opening at a political rally in favor of something much more direct. "For the past four weeks, I have traveled the length and breadth of Wales joining with local party members at a series of fight-back meetings. I have been asking everyone a simple, solitary question and I repeat it here: Do we want to win? Not—'Yes, of course we do.' Or 'OK, why not?' No. I mean do we really, really want to win? Do we really, really want our Labour government back in power?"

- **ATTENTION-GETTERS** – Opening with a startling statement or fact that clearly demonstrates the speaker knows the issues and which will grab the audience's attention. Kenneth Lewis, the former CEO of Bank of America, began a sobering speech to the Boston College Chief Executives' Club this way: "Today, as I stand here before you, Americans are in the economic fight of our lives. It has taken time and pain to get us this far. More time—and more pain—will be required."

3. Is the right person

- **SHARING THE SPEAKER'S BACKGROUND** – Giving the audience a glimpse of the speaker's own history—perhaps demonstrating the speaker has walked in the audience's shoes or faced similar circumstances—helps tremendously to establish credibility.

- **BORROWING CREDIBILITY** – If you're worried that the speaker's background may not be enough, you can borrow credibility from others by telling the audience that the speaker has spoken to others who do have credibility and sought input from them. Sometimes, credibility can be borrowed simply by being on the same stage with someone the audience admires.

4. Is warm and personable

- **HUMOR** – Light humor, especially self-deprecating humor, is often an effective way to show warmth. Former speechwriter, columnist and Pulitzer Prize-winner William Safire began a talk to his college classmates this way: "I entered Syracuse University with the class of '51, dropped out after two years, and am finally receiving my degree with the class of '78. There is hope for slow learners."

- **PERSONAL STORIES** – Brief anecdotes from the speaker's life can be useful to establish personality.

- **SHARE QUOTES** – Quoting someone in the opening can introduce some quick humor or homespun wisdom which the audience will transfer to the speaker.

- **COMPLIMENTS** – Paying the audience or sponsoring organization an honest compliment is a good way to gain favorability. Every organization of people likes to feel it is special; reinforce that feeling and gain favorability at the very beginning.

Lee Iacocca, who made his mark as a businessman by bringing Chrysler back from the brink of disaster, was one of the best speechmakers of the 20th century. He was direct. He was funny. He always spoke to his audience and their needs. And he had great openings that demonstrated the warmth and depth of his personality while also paying tribute to the audience. Those attributes were on full display when he made remarks at the U.S. Naval War College:

> Thank you, Admiral. And good evening to all of you. It's a real honor for me to be here. Of course, I know this place by reputation. Wow, I'm glad to have a chance to get to know it firsthand.
>
> I jumped at the invitation to come for a couple of reasons. First, I tried like hell to get into the service in the days right after Pearl Harbor, but nobody would take me. Not the Air Corps, not the Army, not you guys. Nobody wanted a skinny kid just getting over rheumatic fever. I kept waiting to hear from you. Finally, 50 years late, I get the call.
>
> And after all this time, I guess it's a good thing for all of us that you just want to hear me talk—not fight!
>
> Secondly, I know about the contribution that this institution has made to national security over the years. You've helped the Navy and the country understand the threats to that security, and how to deal with them.
>
> I just wish there was a place like this to do the same thing for our national competitiveness. But believe it or not, there isn't. And that's what I want to talk to you about tonight.

The Main Body

Although this portion of your talk represents the largest part of a speech—70 to 75 percent—writing it should be the easiest. By this point, you've already established the majority of the Body of the speech in the preceding work when you chose the key messages and the structure. Insert them now, make sure they connect with the opening, and simply connect the dots between the key messages.

Don't worry if the body doesn't sound like a speech yet. Don't worry if it seems dry or impersonal. Those are separate chores we perform later. The goal right now is to simply put the main messages and support points on paper—along with the Opening—and keep the writing moving forward.

The Close

The end of the speech should, in all cases, be simple and direct, taking no more than 10 percent of the total speaking time. This is not the place to drop in additional information you couldn't fit in earlier. It should be the place where you sum up the key points, praise the audience for its part and shut up.

The best types of closings are those that remind the audience of the main ideas and, when appropriate, suggest some type of action. One very effective type of close is to play off the opening by creating a circular story that takes the audience all the way back to the beginning. Reminding them of a quote used in your open, for example, gives you the opportunity to revisit and reframe the same quote. Perhaps you can look at it in a different light or use another enlightening quote from the same person. You can do the same with stories and anecdotes.

Here's how Alan Alda used this approach to close his commencement speech at Connecticut College:

> Well, those are my parting words as today's door closes softly between us. There will be other partings and other last words in our lives so if today's lingering at the threshold didn't quite speak the unspeakable, maybe the next one will.
>
> I'll let you go now. So long, be happy.
>
> Oh, by the way, I love you.

Veteran speaker Jim McNerney Jr., chairman, president and CEO of Boeing, provides us another example of a great close. In a speech at the Chief Executives' Club in Boston a few years ago, he spoke about globalization, energy and the environment. He closed his speech by 1) signaling he was near the end; 2) succinctly summarizing his main points; and 3) ending the speech.

> OK, I'm close to the end now and I've covered a lot of ground from the launch pad of globalization. If you remember nothing else of what I've said, I hope you will consider action in support of three things:
>
> One: Ask your congressional representatives to support the pending free-trade agreements with South Korea, Colombia and Panama.
>
> Two: Help our leaders in the United States define a national energy policy—one that not only more aggressively and sustainably harvests traditional resources of energy but also encourages and rewards innovation in the development of new and nontraditional sources.
>
> And three: If you get the opportunity, help argue for a modernization of our air traffic management system as a smart investment for our environment and our energy independence.

Finally, in the same spirit that I ask for your help in these three areas, I also request your support of education initiatives in science and technology. In the U.S. (and around the world, for that matter) there is a critical shortage of scientists, engineers and other technical talent. And the U.S. trend is worse than many other places in the world. Our competitiveness and productivity as a nation—and our ability to produce new workers and retrain current workers for the high-skilled high-wage jobs of the future—depend on it. We are a nation of innovation like none this world has ever seen. Yet we are falling behind in education and putting our technological leadership at risk. But that's a topic and a speech for another day! Thank you, and I'll be happy to entertain a few of your questions.

The exact way you choose to close will vary based on what type of talk you're writing. Here are the five types of talks based on the Communication Hierarchy, along with some tips on how to write an effective close:

- **INFORMATIVE** – Conclude with a simple summary of what you told them, perhaps with a handout of the most important material. If you presented a lot of material, help the audience by summarizing it to two or three main takeaway points.

- **CREATING UNDERSTANDING** – The conclusion should again be simple and direct, reinforcing the key messages in a nonconfrontational way. Another effective way to write a close for this talk (or any of those below) is to visualize the future as you've framed it. What are the consequences of adopting the ideas versus not adopting them? Answer the question: What could be?

- **REINFORCING SHARED VALUES** – Simply reiterating that the speaker shares the audience's values—that's why the person is speaking, after all—goes a long way to close a difficult talk like this. It's often effective here to loop back to an earlier story and close on that. Another way to close here is to use a separate, well-known story and relate that back to your main topic. If the story is shared and loved by many audience members, it's a good way to remind them of the common bonds that unite them.

- **CHANGING ATTITUDES** – If the speaker and the audience already share common values—a prerequisite for this speech—this is a good time to issue a challenge. The CEO of Weyerhaeuser Co., Dan Fulton, offers us an example from a speech he delivered to the Rotary Club of Seattle a few years ago. He was trying to get the audience to accept his notion that the real world doesn't work as an "either/or" proposition and that progress often comes from finding the middle ground. He acknowledges the difficulties the nation faces, then closes with a challenge. "So, it is with a sense of optimism that I'd like each of us to leave today. We're all capable of rising to the challenge in front of us. To do so, we must move past the polarizing dichotomies of over-simplification. We must all work hard to release the potential in ourselves and each other. ... We must all come together to work constructively to uncover new truths and create new beginnings."

- **ELICITING ACTION** – Again, issuing a challenge is often the most effective way to end this kind of speech. A simple, declarative question asking for their support—along with strong action words—can make this a rabble-rousing kind of speech and very effective when done properly. In addition, since most audience members will be ready for the end of the speech, this is a good time to use short—sometimes repetitive—sentences that increase the energy and tension. Finally, remember that you should be able to state in a single sentence what you want the audience to do.

Monroe's Motivated Sequence

The Opening-Body-Close isn't the only way to structure a speech. It may not even be the best for you. Another structure that's highly effective—especially for persuasive speeches—is called Monroe's Motivated Sequence.

Alan H. Monroe developed this model on the basis of a very simple fact: People have needs that must be met. As Abraham Maslow described in his groundbreaking 1943 paper "A Theory of Human Motivation," there are five basic needs inherent in human beings:

- **BASIC PHYSIOLOGICAL NEEDS** – food and sleep

- **SAFETY NEEDS** – security of body (shelter), of family, of employment and property

- **BELONGING** – friendship, being a part of a group, love

- **ESTEEM** – self-esteem, confidence and respect by others

- **SELF-ACTUALIZATION** – which deals with achieving individual potential

Monroe recognized that when these needs are threatened—or perceived to be threatened—people seek out solutions. In other words, they are motivated to look for new ways to protect or even restore a need. He also devised a sequence of steps—a structure—that allows speakers to tap into this very human condition and effectively deliver a persuasive speech.

There are five steps to Monroe's Motivated Sequence and you will probably see very quickly the overlap with the Opening-Body-Close structure. His five steps are:

1. **ATTENTION STEP** – which allows the speaker to establish that he or she has something interesting to say

2. **NEED STEP** – where the speaker describes the need or needs that are being threatened

3. **SATISFACTION STEP** – during which the speaker proposes a solution

4. **VISUALIZATION STEP** – which allows the speaker to paint a picture of the future if the solution is implemented

5. **ACTION STEP** – where the speaker tells the audience what they must do to help protect or restore the threatened need

Let's look at each step in more detail and examine a speech that uses this structure to great effect. The speech is by Benjamin Netanyahu, the prime minister of Israel, and was delivered to the United Nations in September of 2009. He took to the podium to argue that a recent U.N. report, critical of a recent Israeli action, should be dismissed and that the U.N. should condemn Hamas and its supporters.

Attention Step

All of the steps are critical, of course, but you'll never get started unless the audience is paying attention. So it's worth your time to spend a good amount of energy making sure the audience's eyes and ears are all aimed toward your speaker. How? There are a variety of ways:

* Use an interesting quote or shocking statistic.

* Begin with a story.

* Use a hard, rhetorical question.

* Use your speaker's character (ethos) to pull the audience in.

* Make sure the person introducing your speaker sets him or her up the right way by giving the audience a sense of the need being addressed.

* Humor can work but is difficult. It must be original and unforced.

* Use a teaser by sharing something with the audience and then promising to show how it relates at the end of your talk.

Here's the way Netanyahu grabbed attention at the U.N. in the first minute of his speech. Notice how he skips the traditional pleasantries and delivers a direct, eye-opening message:

> The United Nations was founded after the carnage of World War II and the horrors of the Holocaust. It was charged with preventing the recurrence of such horrendous events. Nothing has undermined that central mission more than the systemic assault on the truth. Yesterday, the president of Iran stood at this very podium, spewing his latest anti-Semitic rants. Just a few days earlier, he again claimed that the Holocaust is lie.

Need Step

This is where the speaker outlines the common need being threatened. This is not the time for ambiguity. The speaker must be able to state what the urgent problem is. Doing so allows the speaker to tap into the audience's emotions where most decisions are made. Remember Dale Carnegie, the self-help guru, who said: "When dealing with people, remember you are not dealing with creatures of logic, but with creatures of emotion."

It's not enough to say there is a problem, of course. This is also the step where you display the truth. So you use proof points to help make your case. Proof points can consist of select statistical data and facts (notice I said "select" data—too many numbers will overwhelm the audience), anecdotal stories and illustrations, and even testimony.

After describing how the U.N. allowed someone to use its podium to denounce the Holocaust as a lie, for example, Netanyahu used the safety need from Maslow's hierarchy to show them why they share a common problem.

> Perhaps some of you think that this man and his odious regime threaten only the Jews. You're wrong. History has shown us time and again that what starts with attacks on Jews eventually ends up engulfing many others. … Wherever they can, they impose a backward regimented society where women, minorities, gays or anyone not deemed to be a true believer is brutally subjugated.

Satisfaction Step

This is the traditional body of the speech where the speaker—having outlined a common problem—offers a solution. Now that the audience is motivated to hear, the speaker must deliver a sensible approach. Everything that applies to the body of the speech above applies here.

The solution must be logical and the audience must be able to follow it. Good structures to use during this step, are: numbered lists, pro-con and elimination. Stay focused during this step, resist the temptation to "throw the kitchen sink" at the audience, and make sure it's something they can either implement themselves or support. That is critical for the next step.

Netanyahu, in his U.N. speech, argues for a very simple solution: that a recent U.N. report critical of Israel should be rejected because not doing so would give implicit support to terrorists.

> If this body does not reject this report, it would send a message to terrorists everywhere: Terror pays; if you launch your attacks from densely populated areas, you will win immunity. And in condemning Israel, this body would also deal a mortal blow to peace.

Visualization Step

After outlining a logical solution, the speaker should help the audience visualize the future after the solution is implemented. It's not only important to show that the need will be protected but that the audience will be better off because of this solution. The visualization must seem probable. And it will be stronger if you can tap into audience emotions.

There are three basic ways to help the audience visualize the future.

* **THE POSITIVE APPROACH** – which helps the audience picture themselves successfully in the future.

* **THE NEGATIVE APPROACH** – which describes the situation that could occur if the speaker's solutions are not followed.

* **THE CONTRAST APPROACH** – which allows the speaker to paint an "either-or" scenario. In this case, it's always best to paint a negative picture first and leave the audience with a positive impression.

Here's how Netanyahu helps the U.N. visualize the future:

> As deeply connected as we are to this land, we recognize that the Palestinians also live there and want a home of their own. We want to live side by side with them, two free peoples living in peace, prosperity and dignity. But we must have security. The Palestinians should have all the powers to govern themselves except those handful of powers that could endanger Israel. That is why a Palestinian state must be demilitarized. We don't want another Gaza, another Iranian-backed terror base abutting Jerusalem and perched on the hills a few kilometers from Tel Aviv. We want peace.

Action Step

This is the traditional Call to Action, where the speaker demonstrates how the audience can make the solution become a reality and help them secure their own needs. This step must be as direct as possible. One sentence. Write it down. If you can't write it in one sentence, you don't have a call to action.

One of the best techniques is to circle the speech back to the beginning and use that as a reminder of where the speaker and audience began their journey. You can summarize here and even offer a personal action plan ("this is what I commit to do"). But the main goal is to translate the goodwill the speaker has generated during the speech into action.

Again, here's how Netanyahu ended his speech:

> I believe such a peace can be achieved. But only if we roll back the forces of terror, led by Iran, that seek to destroy peace, eliminate Israel and overthrow the world order. The question facing the international community is whether it is prepared to confront those forces or accommodate them.
>
> Over 70 years ago, Winston Churchill lamented what he called the "confirmed unteachability of mankind," the unfortunate habit of civilized societies to sleep until danger nearly overtakes them. Churchill bemoaned what he called the "want of foresight, the unwillingness to

act when action will be simple and effective, the lack of clear thinking, the confusion of counsel until emergency comes, until self-preservation strikes its jarring gong.

I speak here today in the hope that Churchill's assessment of the "unteachability of mankind" is for once proven wrong. I speak here today in the hope that we can learn from history that we can prevent danger in time. In the spirit of the timeless words spoken to Joshua over 3,000 years ago, let us be strong and of good courage. Let us confront this peril, secure our future and, God willing, forge an enduring peace for generations to come.

One Last Word: Writing for the Ear

There is an elemental truth that you need to accept before you begin actually putting words onto paper: No one really talks like they write. So when you sit down to write, you should write for the ear and not the eye. There is a big difference.

When people write for the eye—that is, for a document that someone will read—they can afford to construct complex sentences and arguments. Readers, after all, have the opportunity to reread a passage they don't understand or to return to it if they're interrupted by a phone call. Audience members listening to a speech, however, don't have that luxury. That simple fact means that the writing you do for the ear must be different.

There are two big differences in writing for the ear. People who write for the eye are often told to be as efficient as possible. If you can write something in five words instead of eight, for example, do it. The same rule doesn't apply when writing for the ear. In fact, you often need to be expansive. Ideas need room to breathe because the audience often needs time to catch up with what they're hearing.

For the same reason, repetition is almost essential when you're writing for the ear. When you're making a key point, repeat it to drive it home. And then repeat it again later for good measure.

Writing for the ear also must be simpler than other forms of writing. Audiences might be able to follow a long, complex sentence on the page, but listening is hard work and their ear can only take so much. Simple words, simple phrases and simple sentences rule the day when writing for the ear.

Round your numbers and statistics, for example, to make them easier on the ear. Instead of saying sales were "$274,566" for the year, say they "were nearly $275,000." Use contractions when you write, too, because that's probably how your speaker talks.

Finally, try to use fresh and imaginative and pungent words. Because you don't have pictures like TV, you have to paint mental pictures for your listeners. So appeal to their sense of vision, smell and touch while you're also appealing to their sense of sound. ✿

INSIDER TIPS

#1 Openings don't have to follow a set formula. You don't always have to thank the person introducing you, thank the audience and then open with a joke. Some of the most effective openings begin immediately with a story and then circle back to the "thank yous."

#2 One effective way to open a speech is by using a "cliffhanger" story. Begin the story but don't give the punch line or ending. Promise the audience you'll give them the rest of the story at the end. It's a great way to create active listening. Just remember to follow through!

#3 How can you accomplish the goals of your opening even before you start writing? Let someone else do it for you. For big talks in public forums, it's likely that someone will introduce the speaker. Ensure they say the right things by volunteering to write that introduction for them. In my experience, no one has ever refused when I volunteered to write the introduction. It sounds like you're volunteering for extra work when in reality you're gaining extra time to establish credibility for your speaker. You can tailor the introduction to your own presentation and highlight all the right points. More than anything, the introduction should help establish the speaker's credibility and show why he or she is the right person to speak to the audience.

#4 Always write a second close to your talk, one that comes after any Question/Answer period if there is one. When the questions are over, hit the audience again with a second close of about one minute. It should include three items: a thank you for the opportunity to speak, a thank you for their interest, a quick summary of the key message.

#5 Beware of false closings. Once you send a verbal signal to your audience that you are about to finish, follow through by quickly finishing. Any hesitation toward the end will only frustrate the audience. If you have four points to deliver, for example, once you get to No. 4, the ending should follow very quickly. Resist the temptation to use this area to drop in all of the "good stuff" you couldn't fit in earlier. If it was really good stuff, it would have made it into the body. Leave it out, stay focused on your key points and get out of the speech.

STEP 8:

Say It Simple, But Say it With Style

I have never thought of myself as a good writer.
But I'm one of the world's great rewriters.

– James Michener, American author

Politicians are often scoffed at for their ability to talk for long periods of time without saying anything at all. Some have a tendency to confuse high-sounding ideals and hyperbole with communications. But the best politicians know how to talk the language of the people. President Lyndon B. Johnson, for example, always remembered who he was talking to and what their perspective was.

There is a story that one day when he was reviewing the text of a speech, he got angry about a line one of his speechwriters had written. The writer had inserted a quote from Aristotle. Johnson, who was born almost in the geographic center of Texas and grew up in cattle country, had honed his campaign speech on farms and ranches. He knew his audience might be turned off by the reference to this Greek philosopher. "Half the people I'm talking to won't even know who Aristotle was," he reportedly said. Grabbing a pencil, he marked out Aristotle's name and began writing in another attribution. "Let's just say, 'As my dear old daddy used to say ...'"

Today's speakers could learn a lot from Johnson. Doing so would immensely improve the rhetoric being spewed out by modern businesses and organizations today.

For many reasons, speakers often feel like they need to sound smarter than everyone else in the room. They are, after all, leaders. Aren't people just waiting for them to say something important and wise? Don't they need to demonstrate how well-read they are? Shouldn't they remind everyone they know big words and know how to write complex sentences and quote dead philosphers?

Speechwriter Mike Long, director of the White House Writers Group, has a favorite saying about this faulty logic: "No one," Long says, "wants to hear you talk. No one." There is more truth there than most speakers want to admit. People want direction. They need motivation and inspiration. They often beg for information. And they will sit quietly with their hands in their laps while your speaker is standing in front of them and they will clap politely when the speech is over. But hardly anyone actually wants to be there in the room, forced to listen.

Why? Because most people are selfish and impatient. If you doubt, stand near the front of an audience—somewhere off to the side—before one of your speakers takes to the podium and just observe. The attention span they give your speaker slides quickly from high to low in a matter of minutes.

And why not? They have email to check and reports to write. Phones are vibrating on their hips and PDAs are buzzing in their purses. It's the first pretty day of spring and chirping birds are singing in the warm sunshine. Bladders are full and they can think of nothing but their own discomfort. And the speaker is roaming around onstage, laboring on point No. 3 of a 10-point presentation, oblivious to the fact that no one ... no one ... wants to hear it for even one more minute.

The solution? Make them *want* to listen by editing your words into language that is fresh and personal, that has a simple clarity, and that is easy to follow. You saw in the last chapter how important structure is to keeping an audience engaged. But that's simply the first step. There is much more you can do to create active listening, where the audience is with the speaker every step. They'll forget about the emails piling up on their computer and they'll tune out the chirping birds. They may even temporarily forget their own full bladders. The key is to take the time to sit down at your desk with your first draft and fix it.

If you're writing anything other than a three-minute talk, in fact, you owe it to the audience and your organization to ensure you aren't wasting anyone's time with a boring and confusing message. Regardless of whether this is a true full-text speech, bullet comments or a PowerPoint presentation, you must edit the words into a message that's warm, personal, clear and engaging. It's not as hard as you might think. But it does take discipline and dedication.

At this phase, I encourage you to grab a red pen and sit down with a hard copy of your speech draft. You need to go through and mark up the speech to catch all of the language and phrasing that gets in the way of your message. Don't try to fix it all on the go; for now it's important to get into a rhythm of aggressive editing. Be hard on yourself, be willing to kill all of your darling phrases that don't work and, when you've finished with the markup, translate it all back to your electronic copy. This process gives you a better chance of seeing the speech as a whole during both the editing and the rewriting process.

Let's break the editing into three categories. You want to make sure each talk you give is Simple & Clear, Exciting & Fresh and Warm & Personal. Here's how to accomplish each of these.

Simple & Clear

William Zinsser, the author of many writing books, once summed up the problem of complex and confusing writing this way: "We are a society strangling on unnecessary words, circular construction, pompous frills and meaningless jargon."

Verbal communication is often the same way, strangling us with the very words we're trying to use to convince, persuade and inform. Listening to someone else is difficult work. And when speakers give their audiences unfamiliar words and long sentences, they force them to work even harder. Remember that our goal is not bombastic or flamboyant words, but simply to be heard and understood.

One of the greatest speeches in American rhetoric was the Gettysburg Address. Schoolchildren still learn it and we have all—at one time or another—read it as a piece of great historical significance. What is interesting to me is that it is also a model of simplicity. The Gettysburg Address has 267 words. Of those 267, 194 of them are one-syllable words and 53 are two-syllable words. There are only 20 words in the entire Gettysburg Address that are more than two syllables. That fact is, in my opinion, why it remains one of our great speeches.

There's no reason to make your words difficult and tiring. In fact, it defeats the very purpose of the giving a speech in the first place. If you really want audiences to hear and understand what your speaker is saying, you must strip out all of the unnecessary words and simplify the phrases and sentences. Here's how:

- **WRITE SIMPLE WORDS** – The natural quote that springs to mind here is Winston Churchill who said, "Old words are best. And old words, when they are short, are best of all." Small words always work better than long ones. Familiar words work better than obscure ones. Go through your talk with a red pen and mark for replacement every long or unfamiliar word. Instead of saying: *It's a necessity that we utilize every tool at our disposal to ensure a feasible and equitable resolution for each party,* you could say this: *We must use all we have to find a fair solution for each of us.*

  - Here are a few examples of words that you could replace:

INSTEAD OF . . .	USE	INSTEAD OF . . .	USE
Accomplish	Did	Ensure	Make sure
Annually	Every year	Implement	Implemen
Attempt	Try	In order that	So
Feasible	Possible	It is essential	Must
Optimal	Best	Minimize	Decrease
Assistance	Help	Necessitate	Cause
Component	Part	Parameters	Limits
Commence	Begin	Pertaining to	About
Demonstrate	Show	Provide	Give
Convene	Meet	Sufficient	Enough
Employ	Use	Terminate	End
Eliminate	Cut	Utilize	Use

- **SIMPLIFY SENTENCES AND PHRASES** – Just like words, your sentences should be simple without parenthetical material and with few qualifying phrases. Subject-Verb-Object sentences work best. (This is especially true if you're writing for someone who is a non-native speaker. Audiences need time to process the accents. At the same time, this is the same structure most people use to learn a foreign language so it is the one they are also most comfortable delivering.)

- **KILL BUZZ WORDS AND JARGON** – It takes people longer to process jargon and buzzwords. Studies show that even jargon we're familiar with—acronyms from within our own companies and organizations—will slow us down. Pack up the acronyms in your talk, delete the organizational jargon and cut every popular buzzword.

- **REWRITE STATISTICS** – Numbers are difficult for people to comprehend. Sometimes, though, they are necessary. The best way to handle this challenge is to rewrite them into something easier to process. Say you are writing a talk about drunk driving and want to share with the audience the fact that about 17,000 people are killed annually in alcohol-related crashes. That's a big number and it's difficult for people to think about, mainly because it has no perspective. Rewriting and rephrasing it solves that problem and makes the number more meaningful: "Nearly 17,000 people were killed in alcohol-related crashes last year. That means that on any given day, 48 people are killed by drunk driving. ... That's a person every 30 minutes. In other words, in the time I will stand up here delivering this talk, three people in the United States will die in an alcohol-related crash and another five more will be injured."

- **STATE THE POSITIVE** – A study by a psychologist several years ago found that it takes people longer to understand a negative phrase than it does a positive one. Rewrite your sentences to take the negatives out. So instead of saying: "I'll never forget," for example, say "I'll always remember."

- **USE REPETITION AND AMPLIFICATION** – This sounds counterintuitive but sometimes we have to expand a point to make it clearer. Like the example above with statistics, you can restate a point to drive it home for your audience. In fact, repetition and amplification is necessary in oral presentations because audiences may not hear what you said the first time. If it is a key message and important enough to say once, then it's important enough to say again. Drive the point home. Use a sledgehammer if necessary.

- **USE EXAMPLES** – A good example can make a particular point come alive for your audience because it amplifies and gives credibility to your arguments. Lt. Gen. William Caldwell, IV gave a speech titled *Leadership in a Time of Crisis* as part of the Lincoln Lecture Series at the University of Saint Mary a few years ago. It was the kind of speech that was made for examples and Caldwell used several. One of his points is that leaders must demonstrate discipline, just as President Lincoln did in dealing with one of his Civil War generals who was failing to act as aggressively as Lincoln had hoped. Caldwell uses a story from one of Lincoln's friends, Ozias M. Hatch, to demonstrate how the president dealt with inaction in his subordinates.

> Another instance of dealing with inaction reported by O.M. Hatch was a dispatch from Lincoln to McClellan that reads: "If you don't intend to use the army, won't you lend it to me?" McClellan replied that his horses were too fatigued to conduct offensive operations. Lincoln wrote back: "What has your cavalry been doing since the battle of Antietam that would fatigue anything?"

Exciting & Fresh

One of the hallmarks of a good talk—one that encourages active listening—is to say something that is fresh, fun and exciting. A lot of people hesitate here because they believe "exciting and fresh" isn't them ... that they don't want their words to sound too much like a political speech.

Keep in mind, however, that politicians these days are professional speakers. They've received training and they know what works. They know the kinds of phrases that excite the listener's ear and they know, most of all, how to avoid the dreadful monotone, predictable sentence structure that puts audiences to sleep.

Speechwriters in every field can learn from them. And why not? Today's politicians stand on the shoulders of the master rhetoricians of the past who developed the first formal study in this area. Like us, they were mostly interested in persuasion. And they, like professional speakers today, knew the power of using the right phrase or rhetorical device.

A few simple editing changes, using some of the examples below, can go a long way to help make your writing more powerful. They'll help you emphasize certain words, help you stress certain memorable phrases and, most of all, help create an audience of listeners who do, in fact, want to listen because the words you've written are fresh and exciting. Here are a few editing suggestions you can use to achieve that.

- **ASK RHETORICAL QUESTIONS** – A good rhetorical question ("Why have we done this to ourselves?" "How did we get to this point?") is a good way to do three things at once. It breaks up the language by changing the tonal pattern, it wakes an audience up by changing the speech's cadence, and it gives the talk room to breathe. Ask the question, write in a good three-second pause and then continue. You'll be amazed at how many of the audience are now looking where they should—at the speaker.

- **INSERT A RHYTHMIC TRIAD** – For some reason, hearing things in sets of three is stimulating and satisfying. We use it to teach children (stop ... drop

... and roll). We use it to talk about popular culture (sex, drugs and rock and roll). We even have the holy trinity, the three wise men and "the sun, the moon and the stars." Successful speakers have known about our affinity for groups of three for a long time and used it to their advantage. Lincoln used it in the Gettysburg Address—"of the people, by the people, for the people"— and Churchill used it during World War II—"never flinch, never weary, never despair." President Roosevelt said, "Here is one-third of a nation ill-nourished, ill-clad, ill-housed." Ted Kennedy said, "On this foundation, we have defined our values, refined our policies and refreshed our faith." Rework your phrases to include one or more of these rhythmic triads. In terms of making your speech a pleasure to hear, it's one of the easiest, most fun and most effective devices you can use. (See last sentence for an example.)

- **USE DUAL CONSTRUCTIONS** – Like a one-two shot to the stomach, a good dual construction can get an audience's attention very quickly. Again, these sentences change the cadence and prevent the talk from being sing-songy and predictable. Former British Prime Minister Tony Blair used them a lot and gives us a couple of examples from this speech given just weeks after 9/11.

  - "We were with you at the first. We will stay with you at the end."

  - "Europe is not a threat to Britain. Europe is an opportunity."

  - "Whatever the dangers of the action we take, the dangers of inaction are far, far greater."

- **VARY THE SENTENCE LENGTH** – A long sentence, followed by one or two short sentences, helps change the pace and rhythm of your words. Actively look for opportunities to write a variety of sentence lengths. Be especially sensitive to two or more consecutive long sentences.

- **EMBRACE WORD PLAYS** – A little fun now and then is good for the audience. Plus, it can often be memorable. Jesse Jackson does this with great effect as in his 1992 speech in Indiana when he said what the nation requires is "not a new savior but a new behavior." Another example: The economy went from dot.com to dot.bomb.

  - **ALLOW ALLITERATION, ALWAYS** – Alliteration, repeating the same sound at the beginning of several successive words, is fun for the audience to hear. Look for ways to judiciously use this technique. Don't overdo it, but a little rhyme every now and then works well for a tired audience. Jesse Jackson was a master at this and his rhymes often formed the backbone of his entire speech. They made headlines and helped make him famous— and fun to listen to—as a speaker. Some of his rhymes include: "Today's students can put dope in their veins or hope in their brain." ... "If they can conceive it and believe it, they can achieve it." ... "They must know it is not their aptitude but their attitude that will determine their altitude."

- **ANAPHORA** – This is a favorite of the speechwriting set for hundreds of years for good reason—it works. Don't let the name throw you. You've heard it work before even if you didn't know what it was called. Anaphora is simply repeating the same phrase at the beginning of several successive clauses. Placed correctly in the speech, it can have a galvanizing and often uplifting effect on the audience.

  - Churchill was a master at this: "<u>We shall not</u> flag or fail. <u>We shall go</u> on to the end. <u>We shall fight</u> in France, <u>we shall fight</u> on the seas and oceans, <u>we shall fight</u> with growing confidence and growing strength in the air."

  - Former U.S. Secretary of State Colin Powell provides another example in this commencement speech at Howard University: "<u>I want you to</u> have faith in yourselves. <u>I want you to</u> believe to the depth of your soul that you can accomplish any task that you set your mind and energy to. <u>I want you to</u> be proud of your heritage."

Warm & Personal

A key part of any talk—whether it's three minutes in front of employees the speaker has known for years ... or 30 minutes in front of new, potential donors for a nonprofit organization—the speaker must be warm and personal. No one wants to listen to someone who's all business all the time. They like to know the speaker has a unique personality. They like to know the person is approachable. In other words, they want to like the speaker. And that takes some effort. But, it can also pay huge dividends.

Some people are naturally warm and full of life and humor. It bubbles through even in the direst circumstances. Others must work at it. Here are some ways you can add material to the speech to show the speaker is warm and personal (even if the person isn't).

- **ADD HUMOR** – OK, it is tricky. And if it's done poorly, it can be disastrous. But when it works, humor can disarm an audience and get everyone in a good mood. So what kind of humor? Let's start with the kind that you shouldn't use. Never use humor that is:

  - Based on ethnicity, gender or race. Don't even try it.

  - A canned joke you got from a joke book or the Internet. If you saw it, chances are someone else did, too.

  - Hurtful to anyone or any organization. Never ridicule. If there's ever a doubt, leave it out.

  - Takes longer than one minute to get to the punch line.

So what does work? A couple of things:

- **SELF-DEPRECATING HUMOR** – A speaker who pokes a little fun at himself or herself is a great way to show humility and openness. But please, oh please, never let speakers make fun of their own speaking abilities. It's the last thing an audience needs to hear. A warm, shared joke about a mutual profession, on the other hand, can work miracles. Here's how Jim McNerney, the CEO of Boeing, warmed up to his audience of engineers at the College of Engineering at the University of Michigan.

  > In ancient Greek mythology, Daedalus built the famous Labyrinth in Crete—and was later imprisoned in his own invention. Ever resourceful, Daedalus made wings out of feathers tied together with linen threads and fastened with wax. Rising on their wings, Daedalus and his son Icarus escaped the Labyrinth. But you all know what happened next. Icarus—not hearing his father's pleas (or, more likely, simply ignoring them)—soared higher and higher. Soon, the blazing sun melted the wax in his wings and caused the feathers to loosen and fall. Though Icarus continued to flap his arms, they no longer caught the wind, and the poor boy plunged into the sea. In the language of engineering, Icarus exceeded his thermal limits—leading to structural failure and a subsequent loss of control. Ladies and gentlemen, students and members of the faculty, that is the wonderful—but unforgiving—world of engineering!

- **FUNNY QUOTATIONS** – Short, humorous quotations allow speakers to be funny even when they aren't because they're simply channeling someone else. They work especially well if the audience is familiar with the original source. These tend to work best when they are recent quotes but even some wise quips from the past—think about the pearls of wisdom from cowboy philosopher Will Rogers here—can strike a chord of humorous truth with the audience.

- **FUNNY HEADLINES** – Many times newspapers or trade publications have funny headlines or two separate headlines that seem to say the opposite things. Relating those can be a safe way to get people laughing. Scan the publication in the weeks leading up to the event and see if anything jumps out. You might be surprised at what you find when you're actively looking. Scan the headlines, scan the ads and scan the photos. The trick here is to be quick and effective and not get bogged down.

- **PERSONAL ANECDOTES** – Brief stories about the speaker help lighten the mood and allow the audience to see the real person behind the suit. These are often the best devices for making speakers seem like real people.

- **INSERT QUOTATIONS** – Many people are afraid to use quotations. They feel self-conscious quoting dead philosophers and political figures. But quotes can be an important part of your speech because they add variety, credibility (especially if you quote someone the audience admires), and humor. By choosing the right person to quote, you show who the speaker admires and that, in turn, tells the audience volumes about the person standing at the podium. Would you quote Albert Einstein or Golda Meir? John F. Kennedy or Jeff Foxworthy? Quoting from Homer's *Iliad* or Homer Simpson? A report from the National Academy of Sciences or the headlines from *The Onion*? Each selection tells a little about the speaker and his or her beliefs. Play with quotes, insert them and use them to warm the audience.

- **DELETE CLICHÉS** – Nothing tells an audience that the speaker didn't put much forethought into the speech more than delivering worn-out clichés. Remove them with a passion. No one wants to hear about how your organization "beat the 800-pound gorilla" by "building a better mousetrap." Please don't tell anyone you've "picked the low-hanging fruit" by "thinking outside the box." Clichés cause instant brain freeze in the audience and should be avoided "like the plague."

- **ADD IMAGERY** – The best talks are more than just an auditory experience for an audience. The very best talks and speeches hit all of the senses and paint images in the audience's collective brain. One of the best examples I know comes from Gen. MacArthur's Thayer Award speech at West Point. MacArthur is talking about the foot soldier and says:

  > In memory's eye I could see those staggering columns of the First World War, bending under soggy packs, on many a weary march from dripping dusk to drizzling dawn, slogging ankle-deep through the mire of shell-shocked roads, to form grimly for the attack, blue-lipped, covered with sludge and mud, chilled by the wind and rain, driving home to their objective, and for many, to the judgment seat of God.

- **INCLUDE "YOU"** – There's no substitution for this simple word in terms of warming an audience. Never speak to an anonymous audience. Speak directly to them by rewriting your sentences to include the word "you." If you don't have three or four "you" words on each page, rewrite. Rewriting to include more "you" words makes the speech more direct and personal for the audience and has the added benefit of reminding you, the writer, that you're writing for individual audience members.

Learning from Others

The best way to learn how to edit a speech is to see how others have done it. Gen. Douglas MacArthur's speech at West Point, given as he accepted the Thayer Award, is a great example of how careful editing can enhance a talk and engage an audience. What follows is his speech in its entirety along with some of the techniques he used to make this talk come alive. There are more techniques than what is listed here, but these are among the most common.

Some of the rhetorical devices used below (and some additional examples) include:

- **EPISTROPHE** – the opposite of anaphore, it is the repetition of words at the end of successive clauses. (There is no Negro <u>problem</u>. There is no Southern <u>problem</u>. There is no Northern <u>problem</u>. There is only an American <u>problem</u>." President Lyndon B. Johnson's "We Shall Overcome" speech in 1965.)

- **ANAPHORA** – the repetition of a word or phrase at the beginning of successive clauses. ("After all, that's what most of us do when we lose somebody in our family—especially if the loss is unexpected. <u>We're</u> shaken out of our routines. <u>We're</u> forced to look inward. <u>We</u> reflect on the past: <u>Did we</u> spend enough time with an aging parent, we wonder. <u>Did we</u> express our gratitude for all the sacrifices that they made for us? <u>Did we</u> tell a spouse just how desperately we loved them, not just once in awhile but every single day?" President Obama speaking at a memorial service for shooting victims in Arizona.);

- **ASYNDETON** – omitting conjunctions between two or more phrases or words. ("But, in a larger sense, we cannot dedicate, we cannot consecrate, we cannot hallow this ground." President Lincoln's Gettysburg Address.)

SPEECH EXAMPLE
GEN. DOUGLAS MACARTHUR
DUTY, HONOR AND COUNTRY
UNITED STATES MILITARY ACADEMY
WEST POINT, N.Y.
MAY 12, 1962

Gen. Westmoreland, Gen. Grove, distinguished guests, and gentlemen of the Corps!

<u>As I was leaving the hotel this morning, a doorman asked me, "Where are you bound for, General?" And when I replied, "West Point," he remarked, "Beautiful place. Have you ever been there before?"</u>

No human being could fail to be deeply moved by such a tribute as this [Thayer Award]. Coming from a profession I have served <u>so long</u>, and a people I have loved <u>so well</u>, it fills

• **HUMOR**

• **EPISTROPHE**

me with an emotion I cannot express. But this award is not intended primarily to honor a personality, but to symbolize a great moral code—the code of conduct and chivalry of those who guard this beloved land of culture and ancient descent. That is the animation of this medallion. For all eyes and for all time, it is an expression of the ethics of the American soldier. That I should be integrated in this way with so noble an ideal arouses a sense of pride and yet of humility which will be with me always: Duty, Honor, Country.

Those three hallowed words reverently dictate what you ought to be, what you can be, what you will be. They are your rallying points: to build courage when courage seems to fail; to regain faith when there seems to be little cause for faith; to create hope when hope becomes forlorn.

Unhappily, I possess neither that eloquence of diction, that poetry of imagination, nor that brilliance of metaphor to tell you all that they mean. The unbelievers will say they are but words, but a slogan, but a flamboyant phrase. Every pedant, every demagogue, every cynic, every hypocrite, every troublemaker, and I am sorry to say, some others of an entirely different character, will try to downgrade them even to the extent of mockery and ridicule.

But these are some of the things they do. They build your basic character. They mold you for your future roles as the custodians of the nation's defense. They make you strong enough to know when you are weak, and brave enough to face yourself when you are afraid. They teach you to be proud and unbending in honest failure, but humble and gentle in success; not to substitute words for actions, not to seek the path of comfort, but to face the stress and spur of difficulty and challenge; to learn to stand up in the storm but to have compassion on those who fall; to master yourself before you seek to master others; to have a heart that is clean, a goal that is high; to learn to laugh, yet never forget how to weep; to reach into the future yet never neglect the past; to be serious yet never to take yourself too seriously; to be modest so that you will remember the simplicity of true greatness, the open mind of true wisdom, the meekness of true strength. They give you a temper of the will, a quality of the imagination, a vigor of the emotions, a freshness of the deep springs of life, a temperamental predominance of courage over timidity, of an appetite for adventure over love of ease. They create in your heart the sense of wonder, the unfailing hope of

- **AMPLIFICATION**

- **THEME STATEMENT**
- **ANAPHORA**

- **ANAPHORA**

- **AMPLIFICATION**

- **ANAPHORA**

- **SENTENCE VARIATION**
- **ANAPHORA**

- **ANAPHORA**

- **ASYNDETON**

- **DUAL CONSTRUCTION**

what next, and the joy and inspiration of life. They teach you in this way to be an officer and a gentleman.

<u>And what sort of soldiers are those you are to lead? Are they reliable? Are they brave? Are they capable of victory?</u> <u>Their story is known to all of you. It is the story of the American man-at-arms.</u> My estimate of him was formed on the battlefield many, many years ago, and has never changed. I regarded him then as I regard him now—as one of the world's noblest figures, not only <u>as one of the finest military characters, but also as one of the most stainless.</u> His name and fame are the birthright of every American citizen. In his youth and strength, his <u>love and loyalty,</u> he gave all that mortality can give.

He needs no eulogy from me or from any other man. He has written his own history and <u>written it in red on his enemy's breast.</u> But when I think of <u>his patience under adversity, of his courage under fire, and of his modesty in victory,</u> I am filled with an emotion of admiration I cannot put into words. <u>He belongs</u> to history as furnishing one of the greatest examples of successful patriotism. <u>He belongs</u> to posterity as the instructor of future generations in the principles of liberty and freedom. <u>He belongs</u> to the present, to us, by his virtues and by his achievements. In 20 campaigns, on a hundred battlefields, around a thousand campfires, I have witnessed that enduring fortitude, that patriotic self-abnegation, and that invincible determination which have carved his statue in the hearts of his people. <u>From one end of the world to the other he has drained deep the chalice of courage.</u>

As I listened to those songs [of the glee club], in memory's eye I could see those staggering columns of the First World War, bending under soggy packs, on many a weary march from <u>dripping dusk to drizzling dawn,</u> slogging ankle-deep through the mire of shell-shocked roads, to form grimly for the attack, blue-lipped, covered with sludge and mud, chilled by the wind and rain, driving home to their objective, and for many, to the judgment seat of God.

<u>I do not know the dignity of their birth, but I do know the glory of their death.</u>

They died unquestioning, uncomplaining, with faith in their hearts, and on their lips the hope that we would go on to victory.

Always, for them: <u>Duty, Honor, Country;</u> always their blood and sweat and tears, as we sought the way and the light and the truth.

Margin annotations:

- RHETORICAL QUESTIONS
- SENTENCE VARIATION
- DUAL CONSTRUCTION
- ALLITERATION
- ANALOGY
- ANAPHORA
- METAPHOR
- IMAGERY
- ALLITERATION
- METAPHOR
- SENTENCE VARIATION
- DUAL CONSTRUCTION
- METAPHOR
- REPEAT OF THEME
- METAPHOR

And 20 years after, on the other side of the globe, again the filth of murky foxholes, the stench of ghostly trenches, the slime of dripping dugouts; those boiling suns of relentless heat, those torrential rains of devastating storms; the loneliness and utter desolation of jungle trails; the bitterness of long separation from those they loved and cherished; the deadly pestilence of tropical disease; the horror of stricken areas of war; their resolute and determined defense, their swift and sure attack, their indomitable purpose, their complete and decisive victory—always victory. Always through the bloody haze of their last reverberating shot, the vision of gaunt, ghastly men reverently following your password of: Duty, Honor, Country.

The code which those words perpetuate embraces the highest moral laws and will stand the test of any ethics or philosophies ever promulgated for the uplift of mankind. Its requirements are for the things that are right, and its restraints are from the things that are wrong.

The soldier, above all other men, is required to practice the greatest act of religious training—sacrifice.

In battle and in the face of danger and death, he discloses those divine attributes which his Maker gave when he created man in his own image. No physical courage and no brute instinct can take the place of the Divine help which alone can sustain him.

However horrible the incidents of war may be, the soldier who is called upon to offer and to give his life for his country is the noblest development of mankind.

You now face a new world—a world of change. The thrust into outer space of the satellite, spheres, and missiles mark the beginning of another epoch in the long story of mankind. In the five or more billions of years the scientists tell us it has taken to form the earth, in the three or more billion years of development of the human race, there has never been a more abrupt or staggering evolution. We deal now not with things of this world alone, but with the illimitable distances and as yet unfathomed mysteries of the universe. We are reaching out for a new and boundless frontier.

We speak in strange terms: of harnessing the cosmic energy; of making winds and tides work for us; of creating unheard synthetic materials to supplement or even replace our old standard basics; to purify sea water for our drink; of mining ocean floors for new fields of wealth and food; of disease

- AMPLIFICATION

- IMAGERY

- ALLITERATION

- REPEAT OF THEME

- DUAL CONSTRUCTION

- SENTENCE VARIATION

- IMAGERY

- AMPLIFICATION

preventatives to expand life into the hundreds of years; of controlling the weather for a more equitable distribution of heat and cold, of rain and shine; of space ships to the moon; of the primary target in war, no longer limited to the armed forces of an enemy, but instead to include his civil populations; of ultimate conflict between a united human race and the sinister forces of some other planetary galaxy; of such dreams and fantasies as to make life the most exciting of all time.

• ANAPHORA

And through all this welter of change and development, your mission remains fixed, determined, inviolable: it is to win our wars.

• AMPLIFICATION

Everything else in your professional career is but corollary to this vital dedication. All other public purposes, all other public projects, all other public needs, great or small, will find others for their accomplishment. But you are the ones who are trained to fight. Yours is the profession of arms, the will to win, the sure knowledge that in war there is no substitute for victory; that if you lose, the nation will be destroyed; that the very obsession of your public service must be: Duty, Honor, Country.

• AMPLIFICATION

• SENTENCE VARIATION

Others will debate the controversial issues, national and international, which divide men's minds; but serene, calm, aloof, you stand as the Nation's war-guardian, as its lifeguard from the raging tides of international conflict, as its gladiator in the arena of battle. For a century and a half you have defended, guarded, and protected its hallowed traditions of liberty and freedom, of right and justice.

• REPEAT OF THEME

• METAPHORS

Let civilian voices argue the merits or demerits of our processes of government; whether our strength is being sapped by deficit financing, indulged in too long, by federal paternalism grown too mighty, by power groups grown too arrogant, by politics grown too corrupt, by crime grown too rampant, by morals grown too low, by taxes grown too high, by extremists grown too violent; whether our personal liberties are as thorough and complete as they should be. These great national problems are not for your professional participation or military solution. Your guidepost stands out like a ten-fold beacon in the night: Duty, Honor, Country.

• ANAPHORA

• METAPHOR

• REPEAT OF THEME

• METAPHOR

You are the leaven which binds together the entire fabric of our national system of defense. From your ranks come the great captains who hold the nation's destiny in their hands the moment the war tocsin sounds. The Long Gray Line has never

• IMAGERY

failed us. Were you to do so, a million ghosts in olive drab, in brown khaki, in blue and gray, would rise from their white crosses thundering those magic words: Duty, Honor, Country.

This does not mean that you are war mongers.

On the contrary, the soldier, above all other people, prays for peace, for he must suffer and bear the deepest wounds and scars of war.

But always in our ears ring the ominous words of Plato, that wisest of all philosophers: "Only the dead have seen the end of war."

The shadows are lengthening for me. The twilight is here. My days of old have vanished, tone and tint. They have gone glimmering through the dreams of things that were. Their memory is one of wondrous beauty, watered by tears, and coaxed and caressed by the smiles of yesterday. I listen vainly, but with thirsty ears, for the witching melody of faint bugles blowing reveille, of far drums beating the long roll. In my dreams I hear again the crash of guns, the rattle of musketry, the strange, mournful mutter of the battlefield.

But in the evening of my memory, always I come back to West Point.

Always there echoes and re-echoes: Duty, Honor, Country.

Today marks my final roll call with you, but I want you to know that when I cross the river my last conscious thoughts will be of The Corps, and The Corps, and The Corps.

I bid you farewell.

- **REPEAT OF THEME**
- **SENTENCE VARIATION**
- **DUAL CONSTRUCTION**
- **QUOTATION**
- **METAPHORS**
- **SENTENCE VARIATION**
- **IMAGERY**
- **SENTENCE VARIATION**
- **REPEAT OF THEME**
- **REPETITION**

One Last Word: Editing Does Make a Difference

There are lots of lessons we can learn from reviewing presidential speeches. But here's a final example to demonstrate the power of editing (or not).

Franklin Delano Roosevelt guided the country through the Great Depression and a World War. Part of his success came from his ability to speak to the people. His language was direct and simple, and he took care to keep his speeches as short as possible. When speechwriters brought drafts to him, he went immediately to the last page to check the length.

Perhaps his greatest triumph in terms of speaking was the Fireside Chat. On at least 28 occasions, Roosevelt took to the radio to talk to the American people in these so-called Fireside Chats to provide hope and understanding to listeners who were struggling through hard times.

Roosevelt was highly educated. He was a Harvard graduate and had a law degree from Columbia. He certainly knew how to talk to other educated people. But he also knew how to talk to the common man.

An analysis of his Fireside Chats show that at least 75 percent of the words he used in those talks were among the 1,000 most commonly used words of the time. He knew the power of simplicity and the power of brevity.

Here's an example of how he began his very first Fireside Chat in 1933. He is speaking via radio about the banking crisis that has gripped the nation. Notice how simple the language is and the simplicity of the structure he outlines in the second sentence:

> I want to talk for a few minutes with the people of the United States about banking—to talk with the comparatively few who understand the mechanics of banking, but more particularly with the overwhelming majority of you who use banks for the making of deposits and the drawing of checks. I want to tell you what has been done in the last few days, and why it was done, and what the next steps are going to be.

William Henry Harrison, however, shows us the other extreme. Elected president in 1840, he made one of the longest inaugural addresses in history. It was more than 8,000 words—and two hours—long and contained a bevy of convoluted phrases. Here is just one sentence:

> Unpleasant and even dangerous as collisions may sometimes be between the constituted authorities of the citizens of our country in relation to the lines which separate their respective jurisdictions, the results can be of no vital injury to our institutions if that ardent patriotism, that devoted attachment to liberty, that spirit of moderation and forbearance for which our countrymen were once distinguished, continue to be cherished.

This speech was delivered on a cold and raw March day in Washington. But the 68-year-old Harrison refused to wear either a hat or coat. He caught a cold, which turned into pneumonia, and he died just 30 days later. There are no reports on how many in the audience died but many were probably dreaming of another life halfway into this mess.

Lesson learned? There is power in brevity and awesome power in simplicity. ✿

INSIDER TIPS

#1 If you are writing or editing a speech for a non-native speaker, make an extra effort to simplify the language and especially the phrasing. Most speakers learn foreign languages with simple subject-verb object constructions. And if you listen closely, you will hear this phrasing in their everyday talk. Mirror that in your writing and you will help them be successful at the podium by giving them language they are familiar with and can handle.

#2 After you've written the talk—but before you send it up the line for approval—read it aloud. Close yourself off in a private room and read through the entire manuscript. You're checking for several things: how long the speech is, whether you trip over any words, clumsy phrasing, sentences that are too long, and ways to improve the pacing. Keep a fresh red pen handy to make notes, rewrite, then read it aloud again.

#3 If you're giving a talk where media will be present, it's important to ensure you say some things very succinctly. Remember, most television stations and newspapers will only use quotes that are about 12 seconds long so you have to be able to get your entire message into that small space. Since most talks are written more expansive than printed prose, it may take a conscious effort to create a complete thought in 12 seconds. It's also smart to make sure that you read and rewrite so key phrases are broadcast-friendly.

#4 How long is your talk? Here's a good rule of thumb. Most word processing packages allow you to get a word count of your document. Take that figure and divide it by 125 (an average number of words people speak per minute) and you have the talk's length in minutes. It's important to know because you never, ever, want your speaker to go over his allotted time. Watch audiences at the next conference you attend and notice how many people start checking their watches as the speaker's time slot comes to a close.

#5 One of the challenges for some speechwriters is when they are told that speeches need to be expansive, but that the writing needs to be crisp and simple. In fact, a speech does need to be expansive enough for the audience to hear the words in real time. That often means you need to repeat or restate important points. That's expansive. But the words themselves should be clean and simple without adornment or pomposity.

Now Picture This: The Right Way to Use PowerPoint

The only certainties in this life are death, taxes and PowerPoint.

– David Murray, editor, *Vital Speeches of the Day*

There's one thing you must understand before you begin developing a Power-Point presentation and that is this: PowerPoint is NOT the presentation. Your speaker is the presentation and the most important element in any speaking opportunity. Second most important are the words you use. Proper body language is imperative. Eye contact is critical. But PowerPoint is not THE presentation. If you accept this basic tenet of leadership communications, this chapter will make much more sense and you will be a stronger speechwriter and counselor.

To begin to understand why this is true, think back to when you were in school and the teacher would stand in front of the room and lecture. Every now and then, the teacher would turn around and write a name or a date on the blackboard. Maybe circle it for effect. And there it stayed, all during class, as a reminder of what you should be paying attention to. Chances are that you wrote that name or date down, too, in your notebook. Perhaps you circled it for good measure. And under that name or date, you jotted down parts of the teacher's lecture—the parts you thought you might need to review later.

That type of interaction is called active learning. Or at least as active as you're going to get with a lecture. It forces you to pay attention by providing a broad topic and then allows you to filter through the lecture for the bits YOU need to know to support it. It allows you to make connections in your mind as the lecturer moves on and this too can be written down if it suits you. It doesn't compare very favorably to learning by doing, but it's not bad.

Now think about the last PowerPoint presentation you attended. Did you write down as much material? Did you jot down those critical facts? Chances are—in fact, studies show—that most people don't do that. Instead, they believe that all they need to know is on the PowerPoint slide. Their entire thinking process, in other words, is trapped within that one box and it's not free to make any type of intellectual leap outside the box.

That's passive learning—and it's a poor way for leaders to share information. Especially information that's designed to do something other than inform.

PowerPoint is also a very "cold" way to present information. It's impersonal and detached. After all, people are looking at the screen instead of a person. So for anything above Inform on our communication hierarchy—in other words, where persuasion is critical—using PowerPoint can lessen the chances of success because it actually undermines the speaker's credibility. Audiences prefer warm and personal; PowerPoint delivers cold detachment.

PowerPoint should be used like the old blackboard. It's merely a support device and you should only write into it the important stuff that supports the speech. Trust your audience to listen to your speaker and make those kinds of solid intellectual leaps for themselves. Let them, in other words, take it from the speaker in their own way and at their own pace instead of having every morsel of information shoved in front of their face.

Financial Presentations are Different

There is one area where PowerPoint—when used correctly—can be a great service to speechwriters: delivering financial presentations. These are the bread and butter of many corporations, the quarterly or half-year earnings reports when all of the financial data is rolled out for analysts and shareholders.

PowerPoint can be a very effective tool here because the audience actually enjoys—and expects—a slide presentation. Graphs and bar charts really do tell a story better than words alone, sometimes. Numbers—which are hard to hear but easier to see—can be shared more effectively. And the slides can be shared across the Internet very easily and left behind for analysts and investors to review later.

Where PowerPoint is most often used incorrectly for financial presentations, however, is when the writer forgets that the same rules that apply to speeches also apply here. Perhaps even more so.

The key points to remember when doing financial presentations are:

- You still have to develop a structure the audience can follow.

- You still have to hone your messages down to three to four key points.

- The credibility of the presenter is far more important than the slides in terms of persuading an audience.

- You must still encourage Active Listening by using compelling stories, fresh language and anecdotes the audience will take away and remember.

- You must strive to reduce noise by making your messages and your slides as simple as possible. Don't let the slides overwhelm the messages.

- You must still find ways to simplify the numbers by restating them in a new way.

- You still have to consider what the headline message is and what quotable lines this audience might take away and amplify for you.

With that in mind, here are some additional tips to enhance your PowerPoint:

TEMPLATES – PowerPoint comes with built-in templates that you can simply open up and begin using. Don't. Nothing screams, "I didn't take time to make this special" to an audience faster than using a template. Templates are like clichés—overused and impersonal. The good news is that making your own personal template is fairly easy. Choose your own simple background color, insert your organization's logo or image and you're set. Simple and fast. If you're part of a larger organization, chances are it has templates you're mandated to use anyway.

DESIGN ELEMENTS – The most critical issue for making PowerPoint a success is simplicity. Keep everything simple: the words, the pictures, the fonts, the headlines. Resist the temptation to fill the screen with several pictures or—even worse—lots of words. A few guidelines:

- **FONT** – Simple sans serif fonts work best on screen. Sans serif fonts are those without the curlicues and adornments at the edges of each letter. Arial, for example, is a great sans serif font that's easy to read on screen. Times New Roman is a serif font that's easy to read on the page but difficult to read on screen. Arial (or Arial Bold) is one of the best to use but other fonts you could use include Century, Geneva or Helvetica. In addition, you shouldn't mix the fonts you use in the body of the slide itself. If you want to use one for the slide title—the portion at the very top—and another for the body, that's OK. But never mix and match in the body. Like using big words and acronyms, it just makes it more difficult for the audience to read and interpret.

- **FONT SIZE** – Headlines should be bigger than the main body and the main body should be big enough for the person in the back of the room to read. That said, you should probably never go below 24-point font size for anything on your screen. If you run out of room, that's a clue that there's simply too much on that slide. Reduce the number of words and phrases. Simplify. Get it down to one message per slide.

- **AMOUNT ON A PAGE** – Less the better. Some designers advocate no more than six words on each slide and no more than six lines per slide. That's not bad advice but sometimes difficult to follow. At the very least, however, keep the messages on your slides as simple as possible. Rewrite sentences into phrases; rewrite phrases to single words. You don't want everything in your presentation to be on the slide. It's far better to use PowerPoint as a roadmap or guide for your audience: a visual clue about where you are in your remarks.

- **IMAGES** – Like words, a few are OK; too many are confusing. If you are going to use images, use high-quality images that don't look pixilated when they're on screen. There are many Internet sites that will lease professional images to you for a few dollars an image. It's worth the money to have quality work. One good technique is to use a single, high-quality photo with a single phrase on the screen that tells the audience where you are in the speech. Think of them as visual guideposts that reflect your speech's structure.

- **GRAPHS** – One of the great uses of PowerPoint is in showing graphically what is hard to describe by words alone. You could say, for example, that after 13 consecutive months of growth, donations to your organization have suddenly fallen. Showing that same information in a graph, however, can be more powerful. That's one reason PowerPoint is used so frequently in the corporate world where a lot of information is reduced to graphs. Unfortunately, there is usually a compelling story behind each graph that often doesn't get told. If you're going to use graphs in your slides, remember that simplicity rules the day. Have as few data points as possible. Make sure it's large enough for everyone to read. And ensure it only shows the key information. And then make sure you tell the *story* behind the graph.

- **TRANSITIONS** – Again, the less complicated the better. PowerPoint will twirl, slide, rotate or spin just about anything on the screen. Don't fall for it, though. It will only muddle your message. At most, a subtle dissolve transition for individual lines on a slide and between slides works fine. Above all, however, be consistent. If you dissolve one line and not the next, it will simply add noise to the presentation and send a confusing message to the audience.

- **SOUNDS** – Yes, PowerPoint does sound effects, too. Again, however, using *Zings!* and *Zaps!* is not a professional or credible way to present information as a leader. Skip the sounds.

- **EMBEDDED VIDEO** – OK, here's one you <u>can</u> use. If there's a video you want to show, PowerPoint will let you embed it directly into your presentation. This can be a simple and effective way to show a video, as opposed to loading it from a separate presentation. Just make sure if you take this presentation on the road or even to a different room, you have the video segment saved as a separate file with your PowerPoint presentation, just in case it doesn't load correctly on someone else's computer and you need to reestablish a link.

Examples: Here are a few examples of bad PowerPoint slides and some good ones

Figure 1.

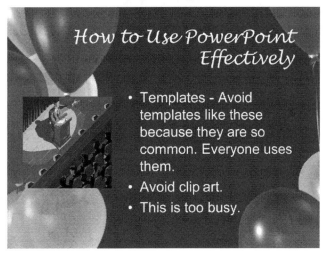

These two slides break all the rules. The backgrounds are templates and too busy. The headlines are difficult to read. The text is too wordy and the image on the second slide is pushed into the background. Plus, the image itself is from the Microsoft clip file. Not exactly original.

Figure 2.

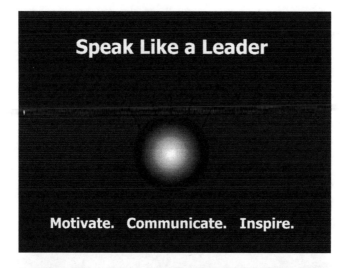

Here are two slides designed with the audience in mind. A simple, uncluttered background. An identifying logo. Simple words and a simple design. If I built the second slide one line at a time, the message to my audience would be overwhelming: simplify.

Even reduced in size here, you can read the messages and understand them.

The Method Approach

There are other ways to use PowerPoint in a presentation beyond what is described above. A lot of creative people are tinkering with the traditional linear format PowerPoint users have employed for years. This tinkering has resulted in a variety of compelling formats that transform PowerPoint from support role to superstar status. They can often be fun to watch even if they aren't the best vehicle to Change Attitudes or Elicit Action. If your goal is to Inform and Entertain, however, you might want to play around with these so-called "method" approaches. Below are a couple of the more popular ones.

TAKAHASHI METHOD – This approach to PowerPoint was developed in Japan by Masayoshi Takahashi as he was seeking a non-PowerPoint way to present information at a meeting. Instead of colorful backgrounds, bullet lists of information and cheesy graphics, he chose instead to use only large Japanese text symbols. Really large. As in most of the screen. Each slide, in a sense, becomes his chapter headlines which he leaves on the screen as he discusses his topic. Adapted to the English language, Takahashi Method slides might look something like Figure 3 below:

Figure 3.

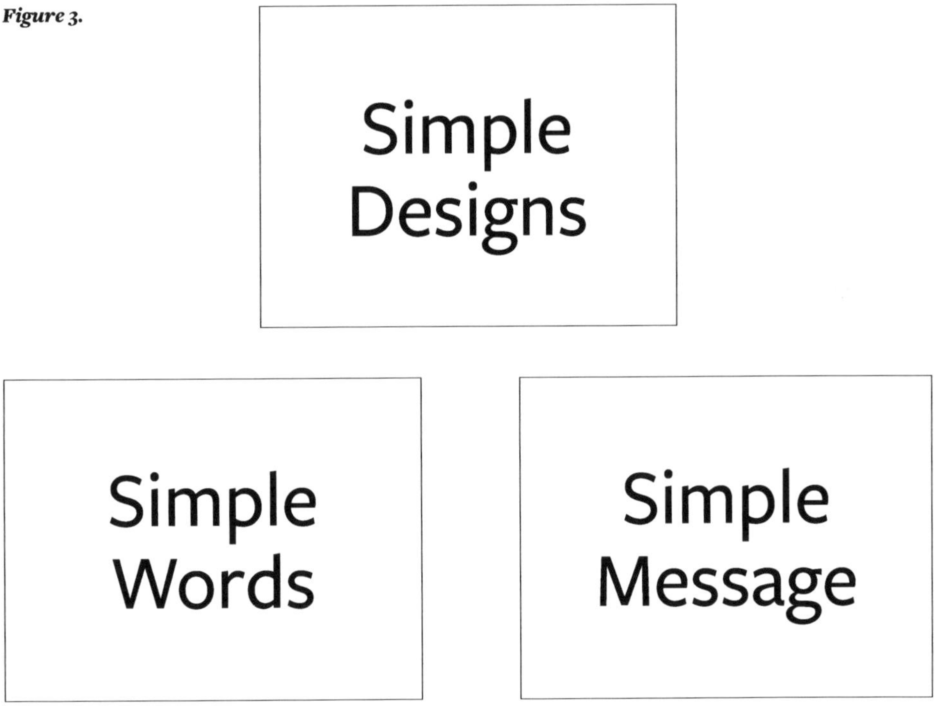

Simple Designs

Simple Words

Simple Message

LESSIG METHOD – Similar to the Takahashi Method, this approach was developed by Stanford Law Professor Lawrence Lessig. It presents very little information on each slide. In fact, most slides are limited to one word or image. The object is to quickly switch slides. Very quickly. The result can be a fast-paced, visually exciting presentation that keeps the audience's attention. The Lessig Method needs too many slides to demonstrate fully in this space, so here (Figure 4) is a screenshot of what a short presentation on the length of speeches might look like using the Lessig Method.

Figure 4.

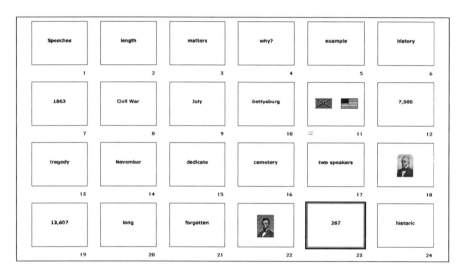

The Lessig Method can be fun to watch and actually fun to present. But there are caveats. It requires the audience to pay close attention to the presentation as opposed to the speaker. If you want to display your warmth and personality and impress the audience with real knowledge, this one might not be for you. On the other hand, if you are a computer whiz who wants to show off your techno-skills, go for it. But be aware that the frenetic pace is a bit like having a white screen flicker on and off repeatedly in front of the audience. While you can present a weighty talk with it, it may seem to the audience that the presentation is more flash than substance. Plus, the Lessig Method requires a lot of work and time to do correctly. A 20-minute talk may require hundreds of slides which are nearly useless as a handout because, without the speaker's words, the slides by themselves mean very little.

OTHER METHODS – There are at least two more "method" approaches to PowerPoint. One, the Monta Method, was developed by a Japanese talk-show host. It uses more text on a screen than either the Lessig or Takahashi methods. Where it differs is in the way it "reveals" the text. Some of it is blacked out—or invisible—until the presenter is ready to show it. In one way, it is very similar to a typical buildup presentation. Where a traditional presentation may reveal entire lines one after another in a linear way, however, the Monta Method may add—or reveal—portions of sentences or images already present on the screen.

Presentation guru Guy Kawasaki developed his own legion of fans and followers by adopting a "10 Slides and You're Out" rule. Almost all of his presentations follow a Top 10 format: 10 ideas and he's finished. As an approach, it allows his audience to follow along nicely and take notes as necessary. Although perhaps not a formal "method," this might be a good model to follow simply because it provides a framework for the audience to follow the talk and focuses eyes back on Kawasaki.

Regardless of what format you use, remember that the speaker is the most critical element of any presentation. Any extra material, whether it's PowerPoint, a flip-chart or even a blackboard should be used to enhance—and never overtake—your message. Keep it simple. Keep it in the background. Keep it under control.

One inescapably strong aspect of PowerPoint—if used correctly—is its ability to help the audience know where the speaker is in the speech. This visible structure is incredibly comforting for the audience. One of the best ways to accomplish this is by using one frame early to set the stage for the two to three key messages you plan to cover. Then simply use one slide per key message as you go forward, maybe accompanied by a large piece of artwork. I prefer striking imaging that relates to the message and covers at least half of the frame.

Using PowerPoint in this way allows the audience to know where the speaker is in the speech but then quickly gets the eyes back onto the presenter (where they belong).

How to Wean Your Speaker Away from PowerPoint

As a communicator, you know that many times a PowerPoint presentation is the worst thing a person should deliver. And, yet, the knee-jerk reaction among executives is that they must deliver a PowerPoint presentation to be successful and, by gosh, it has to look good. I've even had executives tell me they want to do a presentation in a certain number of slides, even before we have discussed what we want to accomplish and what the key messages are. So how do you wean your executives away from this misplaced trust in the power of PowerPoint?

Here are a few ways:

- **RESTART THE CONVERSATION** – Sometimes you have to back the speaker up by literally saying something like this: "Before we talk about PowerPoint, let's talk a little about the story you're trying to tell." This is a great way to reframe the discussion away from tactics and back to strategy where it belongs. (Most executives will understand—and appreciate—if you talk about strategy vs. tactics.) PowerPoint is just one tool you can use to communicate so before you discuss the How, you should restart the conversation back to the What and the Why.

- **USE PEER PRESSURE** – Find out what your speaker's peers at competing companies (or even across the hallway) are doing and find one or two who are giving traditional, non-PowerPoint speeches. Use every opportunity to send along a few clips and reports that demonstrate the press coverage they're getting. Show the quotes they are getting in the media, show the *Vital Speeches* reprints, and send along the full text. These are smart people; they will get it.

- **APPEAL TO EGO** – Most executives aren't wallflowers and they didn't get to their current positions by being shy. Remind them that THEY are the presentation and that the organization will be better served if eyes are on them instead of a slide deck.

- **BIT BY BIT** – If they still don't want to give up the slide deck, at least encourage them to cut it back. Recommend they begin with a traditional opening, use PowerPoint in the middle, then close with a few minutes without Power-Point to refocus the audience back onto them and the key messages.

- **GIVE THEM BOTH** – OK, this means extra work for you but sometimes speakers need to see the proof before they'll believe. So at the same time you're developing the PowerPoint, develop a separate traditional speech—complete with quotes, anecdotes, personal insights and humor—and give them a choice. At the end of the day, the full speech will seem full of life beside its PowerPoint cousin and actually make it easier for the speaker to deliver, not harder. ✿

INSIDER TIPS

#1 If you use PowerPoint on equipment you've never used before, be prepared. First, save it as a PowerPoint show, instead of a normal file. That will preserve your fonts, spacing and animation regardless of the system you use. Then take a backup, saved normally, that you can modify if you need to. Save it on a CD, your laptop AND a portable memory stick. Making copies only takes a minute and you never know when having those backups will save the day.

#2 If you've developed a PowerPoint presentation for a large conference—where your speaker will be just one of many presenters—name your file something unique. Trust me, conference organizers who are charged with loading the presentations ahead of time will thank you if you don't name your file something generic like "Acme presentation." They'll get a dozen of those and have to rename each one. Use your company name, your speaker's name and then the conference name.

STEP 10:

Helping Your Speaker Succeed

All the great speakers were bad speakers at first.

- Ralph Waldo Emerson

L et's face it. An effective speechwriter is rarely just a speechwriter. To do your job—which is to help your speaker communicate effectively—you have to do so much more. There's no one else in the organization with as much access to your speaker or who influences that person's success at the podium (and in subsequent press reviews and op-eds) than you. So it's incumbent on you to see your role in a holistic sense and ask yourself: Am I doing everything I can to help my speaker succeed?

Here are a few additional roles you may want to consider:

Speechwriter as Counselor

Your speaker deserves more than someone who simply takes direction like a quick-order cook. "One speech? Coming up. You want humor with that?"

It's your job to tell the speaker what's required to be successful. After all, you're the one who has researched the audience, who knows what others are saying on the topic and who understands all of the elements that go into a successful speech. Go in with a speech proposal in hand (with all of the key messages written down) and help mold the message the right way.

It's often your job to be a liaison with other executives and other departments such as the media team and local community or public affairs groups. Presenting the speaker with one briefing document—including potential "hot" topics and questions that might arise after the speech—is a good idea. Showing that you have already made contact with these other groups helps give your speaker confidence and shows consensus.

Speechwriter as Speaking Coach

It's one of the ironies of public speaking that up to 70 percent of communication is nonverbal. Even when you're not talking, you're communicating. And sometimes what speakers do when they talk—their body language, posture and eye contact—is so overwhelming that the words are never heard.

Part of your success as a speechwriter is in helping your speaker minimize the negative nonverbal cues and accentuate the positive ones. By doing so, you can accomplish two great things: Lessen the chances that those carefully written words will be drowned out by nonverbal actions and increase the odds that your speaker will be seen and heard as a true leader.

How to go about it? First, watch your speaker perform both onstage and in a more neutral setting like a conference room or in his or her office. See how your speaker naturally uses his or her hands and eyes, and then make sure that the person is using those same motions correctly when at the podium. A few things to watch out for:

- Does the speaker "offer up" ideas to the audience? Good speakers will present ideas and literally offer them to the audience with an open hand. The motion—with the arm stretched out and the palm up—translates into greater audience trust. It is very similar to a handshake that is engrained in many cultures as an example of openness.

- Does the speaker make good eye contact? If not, build natural pauses into the speech and offer coaching that these are the perfect times to look up. There are several ways to do this. At the very beginning of the speech, for example, you can write a three-part "thank you" opening. Thank the introducer, thank the organization and thank the audience. Coach your speaker to look up and to the audience after each portion. Another tip to increase eye contact is to insert rhetorical questions that are natural times for the speaker to address the audience. A third tip is to insert the word "you" and coach your speaker to look up and make audience contact on at least those words.

- Is the speaker too fast or too slow? Many speakers are nervous and speak too fast at the podium. Use video and audio recordings to capture this and send it to your speaker. Upon review, the person will see that the speech is going too fast. You can help by ensuring you've written in enough pauses—using dashes and ellipses—to slow the person down.

- Is the body position closed or open? Watch your speaker during the speech and subsequent question-and-answer period and make notes about the way arms and hands are used. At the podium, many speakers will lean over the podium and grip both sides as if to keep it from flying away. Audiences often see this as fear or insecurity. Coach your speaker to keep hands down and shoulders loose. At the other extreme, some speakers will either cross their arms or lock their hands together below the belt (as if protecting vital goods) during the question-and-answer period. This subconsciously tells the audience the speaker is hiding something. Encourage speakers to exude trust and confidence by "opening" their body. Hands should never be grasped in front of the chest or belt, arms should not be crossed, podiums should not be held in a Vulcan death grip.

You'll also, of course, want to encourage them to practice. A lot. Unless it will scare them, remind your speakers that this is not a speech, it's a one-man play. And there is simply no substitute for becoming a better speaker than by practicing. Thirty minutes of practice is better than no practice at all. An hour is better than 30 minutes.

Ask your speakers to practice even when you're not there to coach them. And encourage them to practice out loud. A lot of speakers will think that reading the script several times is enough. But it's not. They need to make sure there aren't any problem words or phrases and that their timing and word emphasis is correct. Plus, if they want to be effective as an extemporaneous speaker—one who doesn't simply read the text at the podium—they must internalize the speech itself so they know it and can adapt as they deliver.

Speechwriter as Scriptmaster

If the speech you're writing is more than five minutes in length, your speaker will most likely need some notes at hand. What form those take is highly subjective but here are a few ideas that will help you help the speaker.

- **TEXT VS. BULLETS** – To speak from a full text or from bullets is a constant quandary for speakers of all sorts—even those who speak routinely. There are a few occasions where you must have a full text. CEOs who speak to financial groups—where each and every word has a potential effect on the stock price—fall into this group. Lawyers, too, may want to rely on a carefully worded and prepared script. But most people—if they practice (and that is the key)—can deliver a short talk reduced to key phrases, sentences and bullets. They'll also come across more naturally. If the speech is longer than five minutes, they may benefit from having a full text in front of them. Most speakers are busy people and, unless the topic is near and dear to their hearts, it is difficult for them to put in ALL of the practice necessary to deliver a 25-minute speech from notes only.

- **PREPARE THE FULL SCRIPT ANYWAY** – Regardless of which you choose, however, it is best if they practice from the full script. Why? Because you and the speaker took a lot of time preparing the right words that will engage an audience. You worked hard to define and refine your key messages and the words that will inspire. Why throw that away? You don't want to lose that. On the other hand, you also don't want your speaker to sound like he's reading unfamiliar material. How to do both? Encourage your speaker to practice with the full text and, if there is time, then reduce it down to phrases and bullets, keeping intact those lines you know must be delivered well. You get the polished edge of a full script but a speech that will sound more natural. In reality, most speakers make a bigger deal of this than audiences do. Audiences expect speakers to use a speech text when talking for 20 to 30 minutes. The speakers are the ones who put unnecessary—and unwarranted—pressure on themselves.

- **FONTS** – The font on the script your speaker takes to the podium should be big enough to read comfortably from a distance. That said, a 20- to 24-point

point serif font (such as a Times New Roman or Palatino) often works well. Don't bold all of the text because you may want to bold individual words later for emphasis. This is highly subjective, however, and depends greatly on your speaker's eyesight, the lighting in the room (do your research) and even how tired the speaker is.

- **FORMATTING** – If you're formatting the talk as notes (as opposed to a full text) don't clump all of the key messages and support points together. That will defeat the purpose of all of the editing you did earlier. Instead, clump them by paragraphs and sections. Pick out a key line and, underneath it, put in the next several lines and segues, key phrases and sentences. On the page, keep a bottom margin of at least three inches. This will prevent your speaker's chin from dropping down to his or her chest during the search for those notes at the bottom of the page. When speakers have to go to the very bottom of the page to hunt for the right words, it does two terrible things: It forces them to lose eye contact with the audience, and it increases the chances they will talk into their chest and their words will come out muffled. Both reduce the chances they will be a success. A few other tips on formatting:

- **NUMBERING PAGES** – Nothing is worse than seeing your speaker drop his script and having the pages scatter across the floor en route to the podium. So make sure the pages are numbered at the top and bottom so you can reassemble them quickly.

- **SENTENCE BREAKS** – Don't break sentences from one page to the next. Keep them together so your speaker isn't searching for the end of the line.

- **PAPER CHOICE** – Use a good paper with some coarseness to it. The typical copy paper used by most organizations is cheap and slick and often difficult to grab. You want something that's easy to pick up and easy to move when the speaker's hands might be moist. Impress your boss by supplying nice, crisp speech paper that is easy to use.

- **SPEECH BOXES** – Consider buying a speech box. These are boxes that allow speakers to place their script on one side and simply slide the pages to the other side when they are finished. It's more appealing for the audience than to see someone flip pages in a notebook. A company called Brewer-Cantelmo (www.brewer-cantelmo.com) sells the industry standard called a Script Master. The boxes come in different colors and even in leather with initials. Order one for your speaker and explain how it's used.

Speechwriter as Fashion Consultant

The old saying is that we should not judge a book by its cover. Of course, we *are* constantly judging people and making decisions about them in split seconds. Audiences are the same way. They will make split-second decisions as soon as they see how a speaker walks to the podium, stands at the podium and, importantly, how the speaker is dressed. Alas, it's often the speechwriter's job to ensure our speakers look good. No one else wants the job. I've straightened ties, removed lapel pins, turned down collars and subtly recommended speakers find a mirror to brush their hair. It's all in a day's work.

Think about this: The first thing many audiences notice about speakers are their face and clothes. Why risk losing credibility because either one appears tired, haggard or simply inappropriate for the venue? It's important that your speaker look good. A few extra hints:

- Conference organizers often hand out name tags when speakers first arrive. But those tags often have a tendency to catch and reflect the spotlights in undesirable ways. Remove them before your speaker goes onstage and save it for later.

- The same concern goes for lapel pins. Speakers often like to wear pins that show their organization's name or favorite cause. But they are often shiny and will "wink" at the audience during the speech. The solution? Spray it down with hairspray or a clear matte coating ahead of time so it doesn't pick up the light and explain to your speaker what you're doing. Your speaker will appreciate it.

- Pockets should not bulge. Offer to hang onto PDAs and phones before your speaker goes to the podium.

- Hair and makeup should be neat. Do your homework ahead of time and make sure you can point your speaker to the nearest mirror or restroom in case you see something that isn't right.

It's also important that they not overdress or underdress. You know the audience so you can help here with a little guidance—a pre-event memo reminding them of the audience, last minute details and contact information—before the event. The golden rule in these instances is to never underdress. Dress like the audience or, preferably, one step above. If the audience is business casual, men should wear ties. If they are in ties, then your male speaker should be, too. Remember not to overdress for the factory floor.

Speechwriter as Event Manager

Want to make your speaker look bad? Forget to mention to her that the room holds 500 people and there's no microphone. Or forget to mention that, to get to the podium, she'll have to cross a muddy construction lot in high heels.

No one else in the organization—no one—will watch for these things. It's your job. So make sure you do at least the following:

- **MICHROPHONE** – Find out ahead of time whether the microphone is on the podium or if it's wireless. Tell your speaker to get there early enough to do a microphone check. Make sure your speaker knows how to turn the microphones on and off.

- **LECTERN POSITION** – Stand at the lectern and see what the venue will look like. If your speaker is delivering PowerPoint slides, make sure the lectern is to the left of the screen as seen from the audience's perspective. Most Western audiences read left to right. You want their eyes to focus on your speaker before going to the slides.

- **WATER** – Make sure there's water at the podium, regardless of whether your speaker has asked for it. It only takes a second and can prevent an embarrassing moment. If the speech is at a hotel or larger public venue, find a waiter and say you need a lowball glass or, at the least, a glass without a stem. (Glasses with stems are too easy to knock over.) Fill the glass with room temperature water—not ice water—and preplace it on the shelf underneath the lectern. Tell your speaker it's there just in case.

- **LIGHTS** – Ensure there's enough light at the lectern for your speaker to see his or her notes. Again, ask a waiter or house technician how the lights will be during the event. Ask for a demonstration before the crowd arrives. If the lights are too dark, make sure the lectern has an effective light that works. If it doesn't, do not hesitate to ask someone to change the lighting.

- **A/V** – If your speaker is delivering PowerPoint, make sure the presentation is loaded correctly and it shows correctly. Look at the beginning <u>and</u> the end to ensure all of the slides are there. If there is an audio component to the slides, make sure the volume is adjusted appropriately for every part of the room. Walk around the room while the audio plays. And then adjust it upward a bit because the audience will absorb some of the sound. ✿

How to be a speechwriter— and survive

The best advice I ever got about becoming a speechwriter? Don't be one!

– *Caryn Alagno, Edelman*

This entire book has been about how to write speeches—determining what to write and how to write it so an audience will listen and understand. And it's been geared specifically to one group of people, the much-maligned, often castigated and rarely understood communicator who writes speeches.

But how do you BE a speechwriter? And, just as importantly, how do you survive in a position that often seems so precarious?

On the one hand, speechwriters are often viewed with envy within their organizations. Most times they are on the front lines, rubbing shoulders with the organization's executives and helping communicate their most important messages. They typically have good access throughout the organization (which is to say that people will actually return their calls), and, because no one really understands what they do, they're often left to sit alone and toil away at the computer until magical words appear on the screen. They are typically—though not always—seasoned communicators and the very best can earn a nice living.

After all, as Ron Kirkpatrick, the veteran executive communications pro at Toyota, puts it, "Most writers and PR people would rather do anything than write a speech. It frightens them."

But you know the old saying: There is no such thing as a free lunch. With the good, comes the bad. Speechwriters can get typecast very easily, for example. Institutional memories are short, managers come and go, and people forget that the vast majority of speechwriters were already very good public relations people before they ever got the job of writing speeches.

Along with the typecasting comes another problem: Many speechwriters get identified solely with a particular speaker or particular topic. And when the speaker changes—or new topical issues come up—the speechwriter is sometimes seen as yesterday's baggage and shoved out the door. (Insider tip: Always make sure you have plenty of cash stashed away just for this occasion!)

So the hard questions remain: How do you BE a speechwriter and how do you survive?

Most people initially get the job of writing speeches because they are good tacticians and solid writers. They enjoy trying to match language to audience needs. They're good at figuring out the right cadences that will stir the soul of the most cynical employee audience. They relish the fine art of building solid arguments that put their speakers in the realm of the unassailable. And they're masters of dropping in just the right flavoring of rhetorical devices that keep their audiences awake without making their speaker sound like a pompous baboon.

Good speechwriters will have those attributes. But Boe Workman at AARP, another fantastic writer of speeches, says they must also have something else: curiosity.

"Be a constant and continual student of the topics and issues you write about, the people you write for and the audiences your speaker is addressing," Workman says. "Understand how what you're writing about fits into the bigger issues that people care about and make sure that comes through in your speeches."

Kirkpatrick adds: "To be a better speechwriter you need to be curious about a lot of things and read and listen to past great speeches. And make your own speeches from time to time to understand what it's like to be on the other side of the podium."

That means you have to have a voracious appetite for content. Reading a lot about the issues that impact your organization is important. But reading about other things—like ideas—is important, too.

It pays to be a student of good speeches so having a few good speechwriting collections lying around that you can peruse every now and then is helpful. Even more helpful is reading—and watching—current speeches. Get a subscription to *Vital Speeches* to see how some of the best speeches are constructed. Go on the Web—especially Youtube.com—and watch a few speeches a week. Find out what works and what doesn't.

All of that helps you be a faster study when new issues come up and a quicker writer—two attributes that will serve you well when the inevitable mess hits the fan.

But Caryn Alagno, the award-winning writer of speeches at Edelman, raises a good point in the quotation above. It's a sentiment shared by a lot of people who have written speeches for a long time.

Speechwriters have to be so much more than just good tacticians and excellent writers. In fact, you might do best to avoid being called a speechwriter altogether.

"No matter what our business cards may say, we are so much more than 'speechwriters,'" Alagno says. "We're strategists. We're communication counselors. We help our principals and the organizations they represent achieve what they set out to achieve. The most successful speechwriters understand this. We're not scribes. And we should never think of ourselves that way."

Workman agrees. "I have often been referred to as a 'wordsmith.' While it's usually meant as a compliment, to me, it is a backhanded compliment at best," he says. "I—and the people I write for—consider me much more than a wordsmith. They depend on me to know what to say, and what works or doesn't work as communication, not just how to say it clearly, concisely and eloquently, although they expect that as well."

In other words, being a good writer and tactician got you the job, but the smart speechwriter will also be seen as a strategist. That means you have to take a more holistic view of the executive communication function and match its goals with that of the organization. You have to understand what the organization is trying to accomplish—its goals and its long-term vision—and use your skills as a communicator to achieve them.

Along that same line, Alagno adds this: "We should also never think of our work product as a 'speech.' Sure, we work in a medium that is unlike any other. But at the end of the day, we tell stories. We advance ideas. Fair or not, the word 'speech' will always have connotations—stilted, formal and staged come to mind. And since there are so very few great speeches in the public consciousness, every assignment carries the weight of having to deliver 'I have a dream ...' brilliance. No wonder so few people choose to do what we do." ✧

Appendix

Recipe for Failure

Once you've finished writing the speech and you think your speaker is ready to stand and deliver, you might want to take a peek at this checklist. It's a recipe for failure. If you check off anything on this list, you might want to go back and review whether this is a speech that can be heard and understood.

Your Speech Might Be a Failure If:

* The speech is only about what YOU want to talk about without any consideration for the audience.

* You've failed to target the speech on the Communication Hierarchy or you're overreaching the audience's ability to do what you're asking of them.

* You haven't clearly defined your key messages and support points.

* You've built the talk solely on logic, forgetting that many audiences respond better to emotional and character appeals than to logic alone.

* You haven't written anything interesting or compelling to keep the audience amused and engaged.

* You haven't created a structure the audience will recognize and follow.

* You've failed to write out the speech in its entirety.

* The speech doesn't include the one element all people respond to: stories.

* You're using PowerPoint for anything other than informational purposes.

* The speech is full of big words and phrases, high-sounding ideas, jargon and difficult material.

* You haven't checked to see how long the speech is and how much time is allotted.

* Your PowerPoint presentation includes 12-point type, slides full of text and graphs that are busy and complicated.

* You haven't checked out the room where the speech will occur.

* You haven't encouraged your speaker to rehearse or you haven't had an opportunity to provide feedback on that practice.

* You forgot to answer the audience's one overriding question: What's in it for me?

Useful Internet Resources for Speechwriters

(P) indicates a site that requires a registration fee or subscription. Those that are listed are top sites, however, and worth a look if you speak frequently.

Anecdotes and Stories

* Academy of Achievement: www.achievement.org

* Inspirational Stories: www.inspirationalstories.com

* The Darwin Awards: www.darwinawards.com

Quotations

* IdeaBank: www.idea-bank.com *(P)*

* Bartleby: www.bartleby.com

Statistics

* Federal Statistics: www.fedstats.gov

* Poll Information: www.gallup.com

* Federal, business and trade: www.stat-usa.gov

* Federal Information: http://www.usa.gov

* National data: www.nationmaster.com

* U.S. State data: www.statemaster.com

* The Book of Odds: http://www.bookofodds.com

Speech Sites

* Vital Speeches of the Day: www.vsotd.com

* American Rhetoric: www.americanrhetoric.com

* History Channel: www.historychannel.com

* Presidential Rhetoric: www.presidentialrhetoric.com

* Library of Congress: www.loc.gov

* Women's Speeches: http://gos.sbc.edu

* TED Ideas Worth Spreading: http://www.ted.com

- Hillsdale College *Imprimis* Archive: http://www.hillsdale.edu/news/imprimis/archive.asp

- Cicero Speechwriting Awards: http://www.cicerospeechwritingawards.com/

- WikiSource Speech Portal: http://en.wikisource.org/wiki/Portal:Speeches

Speech Blogs

- Vital Speeches of the Day Blog: www.vsotd.com/blog

- Speechwriting 2.0: www.TheSpeechwriter.com

34891812R00068

Made in the USA
Middletown, DE
09 September 2016